ABSTRACT REPRESENTATION

W9-CNB-667
$7.00

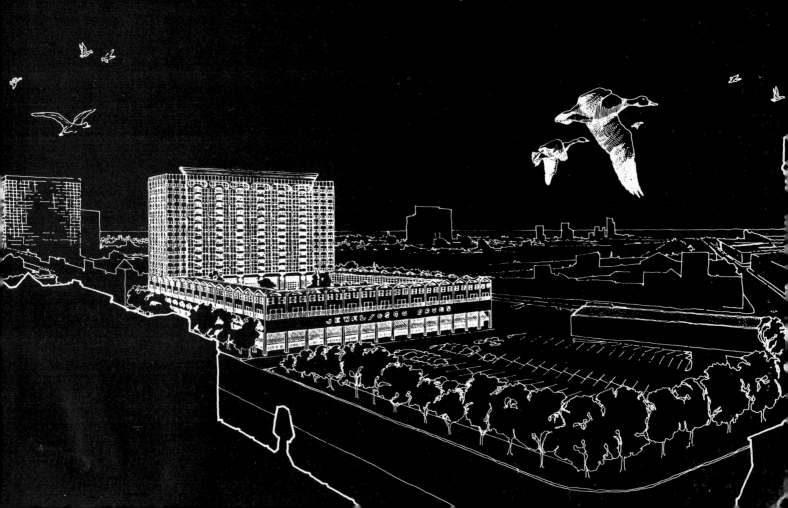

EDITOR/PUBLISHER
Dr Andreas Papadakis

First published in Great Britain in 1983 by
Academy Editions and Architectural Design, 7 Holland Street,
London, W8

Copyright © Architectural Design and Academy Editions
All rights reserved
The entire contents of this publication are copyright and cannot be
reproduced in any manner whatsoever without written permission from
the publisher

AD Profile 48 was also published as part of Architectural Design Volume
53 7/8–1983

Distributed in the United States of America by
St. Martin's Press, 175 Fifth Avenue, New York, NY 10010, USA

Library of Congress Catalog Card number 83–42996
ISBN 0 312 00197 5 (USA)

Printed and bound in Hong Kong

ACKNOWLEDGEMENTS
We thank all of the architects who have contributed material for publication, and in particular Mathias Ungers for having written his article
'The New Abstraction'. Our thanks also go to the many photographers
whose credits appear in the respective captions for illustrations.

This AD Profile was edited and designed by Frank Russell in association
with Vicky Wilson, Richard Cheatle and Bet Ayer.

Michael Graves, *Sunar Furniture Showroom*, Dallas, Texas, 1982, loggia. Abstrac-
ting the sky, piazza and archetypal house in a manner reminiscent of Aldo Rossi
and primitive architects. (ph Charles McGrath)

Front cover
Hans Hollein, *Städtiches Museum*, Abteiberg, Mönchengladbach, Germany,
1976–82. See pages 110–20. (ph Hans Hollein)

Back cover
Michael Graves, *The Humana Building*, Louisville, Kentucky, USA, 1982, model
viewed from Main Street. See pages 101–04 (ph Proto Acme Photo, Princeton, NJ)

Inside front cover
Michael Graves, *The Humana Building*, Louisville, Kentucky, USA 1982. Mural of
the 'Alternative Landscape' in the lobby, showing the Ohio Bridge trusses and a
piazza of vernacular classicism. The lobby itself has the usual Gravesian sconces
with Hoffmannesque relief above and sectioned torus mouldings below.

ABSTRACT REPRESENTATION

Guest-Edited by Charles Jencks

CONTENTS

A.D. Architectural Design Profile

Charles Jencks
The Perennial Architectural Debate

The Eisenman Paradox: Elitism, Populism and Centrality

In 1970, Peter Eisenman wrote a rather puzzling review of *Meaning in Architecture*, a book I co-edited with George Baird in 1969—puzzling because its main concern was not with the book, but rather with an article of mine called 'Pop—Non Pop'. Even this ostensible subject occupied Eisenman only for a second, as he used the review to air a theme close to his heart—the confrontation between Elitism and Populism[1]—projecting this subject rather skilfully onto both texts. At the time this intentional misreading, or 're-reading' as it is now fashionably known, provoked me because I thought it self-indulgent; with the passage of time, and further Eisenmanian inventions (especially his creative fabrication of Stirling and Gowan's Leicester Building)[2] it has become more interesting. For one thing, it illuminates his own progress—a development from elitism to hermeticism to Neo-Academicism—but its main value is in focusing on a very pertinent question: what is the role of the professional architect in a pluralist, agnostic society? If he serves that society, the populist position, his work may perhaps be contaminated by the kitsch of mass culture (to pre-empt a later point of Eisenman, Frampton and Tafuri). Since our culture contains no great belief in anything, the argument goes, and since there are no identifiable clients or iconographic programme, all representational architecture is thrown into doubt. Venturi, Moore, Graves, Bofill and the Post-Modernists are merely trying to resuscitate a dead body. Whereas if the designer serves architecture alone, his work will ultimately become popular (after an initial incomprehension).

The truth of this paradox is born out, it seems, by architectural history. Since Vitruvius and Alberti concentrated on *abstract* notions of design (harmony, *concinnitas*, proportion), since Palladio and Ledoux focused on the perfection of a logical order (independent of semantics), since Thomas Jefferson as much as Mies van der Rohe produced beautiful, and sometimes popular, buildings by the reduction of architecture to a system, the paradox has been apparent if not obvious. On one level, it concerns the transcendent quality of technic or craft, the strange but ineluctable process whereby all means that are taken as ends transform their status from utility into art, an art most often appreciated by an elite. By using grid planning paper—a tool midway between Cartesian abstraction and Durand's formula of composition—as an aid for layout in plan and section, Thomas Jefferson transforms simple Platonic solids into well-organised sequences [**1, 2**]. Note the way the diagrammatic system recedes into the background (the literal grid-lines disappear) to re-emerge as a transcendent expression (the underlying concept). Thus one of the great planned spaces of America is created with a seeming ease and mechanical facility [**3**]. The beauty of the plan resides in both its human scale and perceptibility: the organisational idea is always as clear as a Platonic diagram, yet never as crude or constricting as it has become in the work of twentieth-century followers of this method (one might say *the* method of Modernism, Durand's grid).

The paradox, to return to it, is that an arcane system of reference and an elitist method of composition have resulted in

1

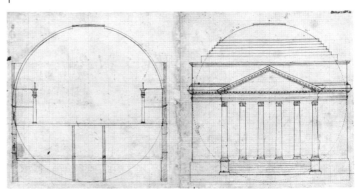

2

3

1, 2 Thomas Jefferson, University of Virginia, Charlottesville, Virginia, 1816–26. Jefferson formulates the abstract idea, the 'academical village' opposed to the centralised institution, and articulates the consequences in a linear, then three-dimensional manner. Professors' lodges, or pavilions, and student accommodation alternate on a line which connects the culmination of culture (the library) with nature (the Blue Mountains) while in back are placed facilities of a less ideal kind: privies, gardens, refectory for eating and learning French. The 12 professors are each given the transformation of a classical monument which is specified in a laconic reference as if it were just another system.

3 Pavilion I, specified as a transformation of the 'Doric of the Baths of Diocletian, Chambray'. (ph Jencks)

a popular place and set of buildings. We may find, in the 1920s, Le Corbusier trying to re-establish architecture as a public, popular art which might appeal equally to 'a Frenchman, a Negro, a Laplander', to 'big businessmen, bankers and merchants' as well as to 'the chosen few'[3] by being based on fundamental types, on Purist universals. His Vers une architecture (1923) was meant both to popularise Modern architecture and to appeal to the new corporate elite; to a certain extent, after 17 reprints and many foreign translations, his message has worked on the contradictory levels he desired. Modern architecture sought to be just as popular as Jefferson's classicism, at least during its heroic period when it had pretensions to transform the taste of a mass culture.

It is this intention which Peter Eisenman engages in his next re-reading, this time concerning Richard Meier's Smith House [4]. The immediate catalyst is an attack by Peter Papademetriou on the imagery of the Neo-Corbusian language containing an idea which Eisenman was later to turn against Post-Modernism: namely that a popular image is necessarily consumerist and corrupt. Papademetriou states in his 'Le Corbusier à la Mode, Revolution for the Sell of It': 'Through a softening of the revolutionary overtones of its sources (Le Corbusier, the Heroic Period), it must appear inevitably as another form of packaging; one either currently available to a corporate capitalist elite or one to be aspired to. The dialectical tensions of Le Corbusier are gone, and the International Style stands before us finally to be recognised as a décor de la vie.'[4] Eisenman answers: 'The point which your correspondent misses is that it is precisely because the Smith House is not avant garde that it is therefore accessible to popular taste. . . In the end, what your correspondent may be objecting to, is that while he aspires to a populism, the Smith House aspires to high art and in the process it may also eventually become popular.'[5]

The paradox is stated directly and in a manner which reminds us of the presuppositions of traditional culture: that high art trickles down and ultimately influences popular culture. Le Corbusier had stated in the 1920s that architects must lead society, create 'a 'mass production spirit' and transform the level of mass taste; by the 1930s he realised that this society was not going to follow the lead of Modernism. In this light, Eisenman's defence of populist Modernism is provocative, for he explicitly disassociates it from the utopian and socialist ideals of the 1920s. In 1971, and for the next four years, he sets his own position and that of the 'Whites' rigorously against functionalism and egalitarianism—twin justifications of Modernism— while at the same time accepting its formal language, not as a décor de la vie but as a superior form of abstraction. This position was enunciated particularly at Art Net lectures in London in 1975 as American formalism versus European social amelioration. It appeared that the Whites, or New York Five, were anti-political, anti-ideological.

In fact this was only a tactical position, for Eisenman at any rate, held for a few years until he clarified his elitism. Influenced by Italian Marxists, Rossi, Tafuri, and French intellectuals such as Foucault, Eisenman started to criticise all aspects of consumer society, especially those concerned with popularity. By the late 1970s, he had dropped all notions of a popular Modernism, consciously embraced a form of nihilistic elitism and produced his most esoteric schemes. By then he had argued, somewhat inconsistently, four different positions: against European 1920s Modernism, against ideology of any kind, against consumerist ideology and Post-Modernism and in favour of a relativistic, nihilistic ideology. One values Eisenman for the extremism, not consistency, of his position. It clarifies what so many feel in an inarticulate way.

In a key text published in 1980, 'Transformations, Decompositions, and Critiques: House X', Eisenman set out a debate between two positions: his former self, represented by the critical 'Voice' and his present self represented by the 'Architect' of House X.[6] Both persona are, of course, concerned with architecture as system, a continuing concern of Eisenman since his student days at Cambridge, Massachusetts, where he formulated the theory of 'linear' versus 'centroidal' organisation. In all cases, whatever the system, it is conceptually akin to an impersonal architectural computer. The programmer, in this case Eisenman, plugs in the arbitrary rules, but the combinations, and ultimate print-out, seem to be independent of author, creator or individual will.

'Voice: the transformations which elaborated the formal structure of House IV and House VI [5] were to a large extent the result of a linear process that at each stage revealed a limited set of alternatives . . . This was intended at the time as a contrast to the traditional design process which begins with an image already preconceived . . . [By contrast here] process becomes the object. The process no longer produces a preconceived object as in a traditional design process, but rather results in the exhaustion of the process when no further steps are possible, when there is a closure suggested by the cumulative direction of all previous stages . . . Even in [this] process of transformation, in which an object is produced from a logical and linear sequence of moves, there is a distance between the final object and the architect, for the object is not something that begins as a fullblown image in the mind of the architect, but rather something that takes on its identity through the process of development. Indeed, in an attempt to be as "distanced" as a computer playing chess, the architect of [Houses I – IX] scanned the range of possible moves with as much neutrality as possible to produce his architectural objects.'[7]

We might be a little sceptical of the sharp contrasts drawn here. Every architect modifies his design in semi-automatic ways, no matter how preconceived his final image; Eisenman's houses all look like black, white and grey rectangles and so must involve considerable preconception. The comparison of architecture to a neutral chess game is an old conceit of classicists convinced of their rationality and impersonality. So it's not a new idea, as Eisenman thinks, and in its automatism is no different from Jefferson's system. Both may produce beautiful, transcendent architecture. There are, however, new intentions and results in this process, which we will return to later. But for the moment the interesting thing is the paradox of the architectural machine which produces sensuality. Eisenman has touched on this in another text: 'My first concern in looking at the nature of architecture involved an attempt to change the nature of the sign of the substance—from referring to man to referring to architecture itself . . . The first house was built like a model airplane—the connections between columns and beams were actually sanded down and glued together. House II was built to look like a model [6] . . . the architectural sign is not like a linguistic sign, since it aslo has substance and sensuous properties. Fundamentally architecture is involved with sensuous properties, rather than merely with relationships of signs.'[8]

Again, we may dismiss Eisenman's reductions (the linguistic sign is sensual) while focusing on the truth of his message: it is a perennial truth. All building 'about' itself transcends into architecture, just as all writing focused on its expressive plane becomes literature. The very definitions of architecture and literature, from a semiotic viewpoint, are made in terms of self-reflexive sign systems—languages which concentrate on themselves while also doing other things. This much is clear and

4

4 Richard Meier, Smith House, Darien, Connecticut, 1965–67. There were contradictory reactions towards this house when it was first published: applauded for its intelligent craftsmanship, it was also faulted for turning radical Modernism into a genre. (ph Ezra Stoller/Esto Inc.)

5 Peter Eisenman, House for the Frank Family, Washington, Connecticut, 1975–76. The house represents a 'process', the method of adding or subtracting squares and pilasters of space. This process is then marked throughout the interior and exterior. (ph Jencks)

6 Peter Eisenman, House II, Falk House, Hardwick, Vermont, 1969–70. 'Cardboard Architecture' was conceived to make the model in the mind of the architect as real as the final house, so the conception might dominate the perception. (ph Eisenman)

6   5

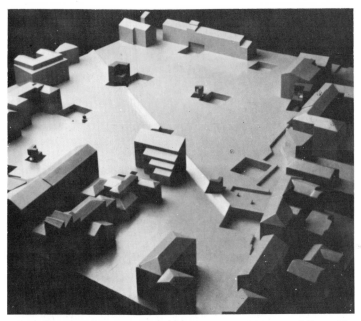

7 Peter Eisenman, Canneregio Projects for Venice, 1980. The use of House 11a, a house on an L, as a model which symbolises deconstruction, the process of designing by analysis, not synthesis.

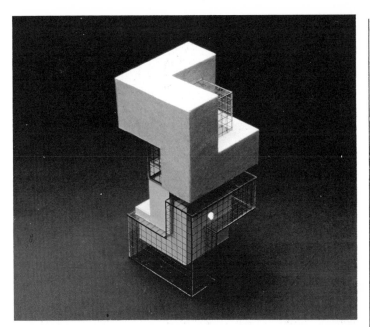

8 Peter Eisenman, House 11a. Simplified deconstruction '... *suggested a more uncertain condition of the universe. House 11a takes this condition of uncertainty as its point of departure... We live today in an age of partial objects ... the whole is full of holes.'*

agreed between Eisenman and virtually all theorists of semiotics and literature. The only problem is the question of the audience; one man's architecture is another man's building. If the self-reflexive sign system is not accessible, it will not be transcendent. Here Eisenman parts company with Jefferson and the classical tradition, and we return to the great debate of elitism versus an accessible architecture.

In the pre-industrial past, culture was mediated by an elite which set standards and formulated advanced or distanced norms. With the Industrial Revolution and the creation of the avant-garde in 1820, the traditional elite fragmented in various ways: professional, ideological and in accordance with taste. In Stendahl's *The Charterhouse of Parma*, published in 1839, there is the notion of writing to 'The Happy Few'; in Herbert Gans' *Popular Culture and High Culture* in 1974, there is the notion of producing for *seven* different 'taste cultures' (formed by class, upbringing and choice). In the intervening period, the 'general reader'—that balanced, widely educated citizen—has given way to the specialist, the person, for example, with an advanced degree in art history whose taste in music is undeveloped. Otherwise, the generalist has been supplanted by the mass audience whose favourite musician is Liberace (the most *popular* on a world level). In either case, traditional culture, which depended on an integration of tastes and knowledge died. In our century, the avant-garde with its ideology of Modernism has been a last, desperate attempt to overcome this breakdown. It hoped to transform mass culture by elevating its ideals, changing its language, giving it intelligent standards. This was the Heroic Period of the 1920s.

It is interesting to see how Eisenman and the current avant-gardes, or groupuscules, relate to this tradition. Eisenman, more than the others, focuses on the history of the avant-garde itself. He has built up an impressive collection of Modernist books and periodicals, and argues for an architectural equivalent of the more 'pure' avant-garde stemming from Mallarmé, which concentrates on the specificity of each artistic language. For poetry it might be pure sound, for architecture pure space, or the purity of architectural elements (Eisenman's white walls, partitions, colours and windows). With modern life—the large concentrations into superblocks and megastructures—architecture has left its previous anthropomorphic scale and represen-

tational role. It has become abstract, as Eisenman says of sculpture: '*Modern sculpture shifted from representation to abstraction and thus from scale-specific to scale non-specific— that is, it became self-referential. How large is a Brancusi or a Sol Le Witt? When sculpture ceased to be anthropomorphic, it became scale non-specific.*'[9] Eisenman goes on to spell out his own abstract, 'scale non-specific' progression: '*The project for Cannaregio* [7] *took House 11a* [8] *and built it as three differently scaled objects. One of the objects is about four feet high, it sits in the square and is the model of a house. You can look at it and think "well, that is not a house; it is the model of House 11a". Then you take the same object and put it in House 11a; you build House 11a at human scale—and you put this same model of it inside ... the larger object minimalizes the smaller one. Once the object inside is memorialized, it is no longer the model of an object; it has been transformed ... into a real thing. As a consequence, the larger house, the one at anthropomorphic scale, no longer functions as a house.*

'*Then there is a third object, which is larger than the other two, larger than "reality", larger than anthropomorphic necessity... It becomes a museum of all these things.*'[10]

This is like Borges' endless library of self-referring books, or Mozuna's house for his mother with infinite boxes within boxes, a paradox where the language has taken over from the speaker, a particularly Late-Modern conundrum. Eisenman drives home the extreme logic as any good Late-Modern painter would: '*Because of the changes in scale, these objects suggest a whole series of other ideas which have nothing to do with the size of man in relationship to the size of the object (whether it is bigger than man, the right size, or smaller). This three-stage process led me to House El Even Odd,* [9–12] *where one begins with what appears to be an axonometric model but which itself becomes the reality.*'[11]

Instead of analysing El Even Odd (a pun on House 11a as an 'odd' one), we might summarise the implications of Eisenman's arguments and development, because they stand for so much Late-Modern architecture in general, and at the highest possible artistic and theoretical level. Clearly there has been the movement from elitism to a hermeticism which approaches solipsism. Yet Richard Meier occasionally builds this kind of abstraction, and there are a considerable number of 'The Happy

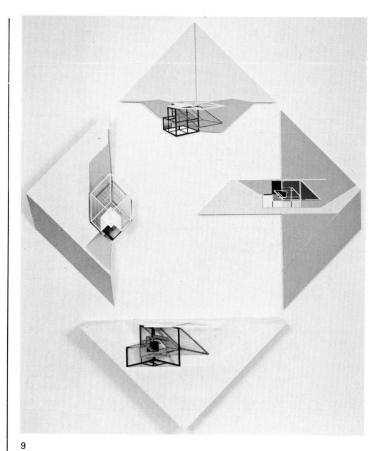

9

10   11

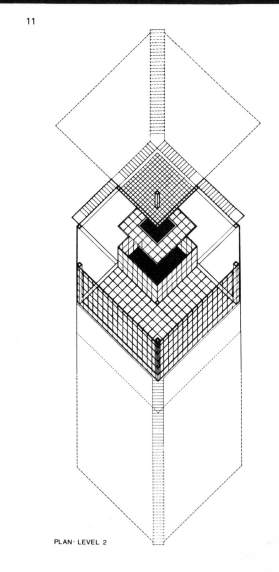

	CUBE	EL	FIRST AXONOMETRIC	SECOND AXONOMETRIC
OBLIQUE ELEVATION				
FRONTAL ELEVATION				
PLAN				
AXONOMETRIC				

12

9–12 Peter Eisenman, House El-Even Odd, 1980. A paradoxical version of House 11a lying down as an axonometric model of its former self so that from everywhere, but one point, it looks crazy, and from the right point it looks correct: ie standing up, which it isn't. Exploring the relation between modelling (or drawing) and reality has been important since the Renaissance, but with Eisenman and Late-Modernists it becomes the content of architecture. (ph Bevan Davies)

PLAN · LEVEL 2

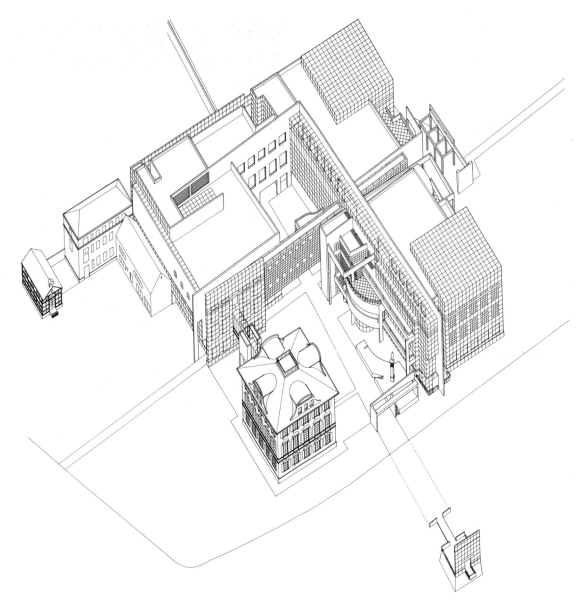

13

Few' who want to follow the exquisite chess moves [**13**]. Indeed, Eisenman's Institute for Architecture and Urban Studies, and its magazines *Oppositions* and *Skyline*, have been so effective in purveying and explicating the hermeticism that it has become appreciated not only by the readers of these magazines (and others such as *A+U*), but also by university professors and their many students. The logic of the New Abstraction is compelling, however esoteric, and it is highly teachable. In short, it is beginning to constitute a Neo-Academicism, with a doctrine comparable to that of the Beaux-Arts, and a system as mechanical as Jefferson's. Could it also then become disseminated, understood and finally popular? Could it act as a centralising focus for a common culture? Certainly not, for there are notable differences between this academicism and those of the past.

First and most importantly, the taste-cultures which appreciate much architecture—that is academia and the avant-garde—are no longer leading ones, as was the traditional, pre-industrial elite. They remain a marginal minority while most of the architectural culture is created by the large offices, the Mid-Cult practitioners, or the smaller commercial practices, which have, perhaps, never heard of Eisenman, nor practised architecture as an art (or certainly as high art). Roughly 95% of the environment is created by this mass culture; by the very masses who Le Corbusier and the avant-garde of the 1920s

13 Richard Meier, Frankfurt Museum, 1980. This beautiful abstraction, now under construction, abstracts certain window features and proportions from the existing museum, then transforms them in the three remaining quadrants, and introduces the 3.5° shift inherent in the site. The quadrapartite organisation, decentred quality and deconstructed fragmentation relate it to Eisenman's recent houses.

wished to reach. By contrast the elite today no longer tries to direct the culture as a whole. The notion of leadership itself is cast into doubt. There is little influence of the elite on mass culture, little 'trickle down' of ideas and forms that is not changed, commercialised and debased. The popular work, the prestige commissions, the largest buildings and those with most impact on the city—in crude terms the best jobs—are left to the Portmans and the Seiferts (or their lesser commercial counterparts). There is no serious attempt to challenge this situation; there is no real assault on the market-place—at least not from the Late-Modern elite.

Secondly, and this partly explains the first point, the avant-garde has little to say which would interest mass society. Goals, values and language divide the avant-garde from society, whereas in the 1920s the Modernists tried to build low-cost housing, order cities into formalised organisms, produce an egalitarian style and transform everyday life. At least they *said* these were the things they were trying to do, hence the label 'The Heroic Period'.

Lastly, with the fragmentation of industrial societies into separate taste-cultures, and with the disappearance of unifying concepts such as the 'general' citizen, the notion of centrality has gone. No serious individual or group speaks for architectural culture as a whole. It is too pluralist and inchoate. The hope, now increasingly vain, is that of the Eisenmanian paradox—that elite values and attitudes will disseminate and become widely popular; that a unified, or coherently articulated, culture is possible. According to another theme of twentieth-century literature and philosophy however—and one embraced by Eisenman by the late 1970s—unity has been lost forever. W B Yeats, in the most often quoted line on centrality, wrote: '*Things fall apart, the centre cannot hold.*' The centrality of European culture, the anthropocentric universe, the centre of the self—identity—have all been destroyed by mass culture, modern science and psychology (to mention only three of the most obvious causes).

Kurt Goedel, Werner Heisenberg, Jean Paul Sartre and Martin Heidegger emphasise the irreducible existence of uncertainty, error, entropy and final nothingness. In place of the classical axiom '*ex nihilo, nihil fit*' (from nothing, nothing is made) is Sartre's and Heidegger's reversal: from nothingness and its spectre comes man's self-definition and culture.[12] A typical twentieth-century character, the protagonist of Robert Musil's *The Man without Qualities*, enunciates the inherent futility of this point: '*These days one never sees oneself whole and one never moves as a whole.*' Wholeness, balance, integration—in short all the interconnections made possible by a coherent culture and all the fictions upheld by the idea of centrality—seem to be gone.

Positive Nihilism and the New Abstraction

Several factors have led Late-Modernists to the architecture they now practise. On the most basic and general level is agnosticism. Since society demands little of the architect by way of representation (except the most basic commercial distinctions) and since mass society no longer has many institutions such as the church or public creeds such as democracy for which to build, the architect is thrown towards abstraction. Absence of belief—agnosticism—produces impersonal design, and the increasing power of other media (TV, newspapers, advertisements) have made this the norm.

On a higher level than this pervasive approach—now the style of most corporations and corporate practitioners—is the *representation* of this abstraction, the self-conscious understanding of this agnosticism, and its generalisation to an extreme, to a nihilism which is positive. Note the difference. Architects such as Peter Eisenman, Aldo Rossi and Rafael Moneo don't simply betray an absence of belief, which is agnosticism, but rather they represent symbolically the belief in absence, nullity and non-existence [14]. Indeed, in a daring re-reading of history in 1976, Eisenman tried to redefine Modernism in terms of this metaphysic: '*It is true that sometime in the nineteenth century, there was indeed a crucial shift within Western consciousness: one which can be characterised as a shift from humanism to modernism. . . In brief, the modernist sensibility has to do with a changed mental attitude towards the artifacts of the physical world. . . It is displayed in the non-objective abstract painting of Malevich and Mondrian; in the non-narrative, atemporal writing of Joyce and Apollinaire; the atonal and polytonal compositions of Schönberg and Webern; in the non-narrative films of Richter and Eggeling. . . Abstraction, atonality, and atemporality, however, are merely stylistic manifestations of modernism. . . [They] suggest a displacement of man away from the center of his world. He is no longer viewed as an* originating

14 Rafael Moneo, *Logroño Town Hall*, Spain, 1980–82. The absent classical language is symbolised by the Neo-Tuscan blank walls. Moneo has written very perceptively of Rossi's use of minimal signs and memory in the Modena Cemetery.

agent. *Objects are seen as ideas independent of man. . . Modernism, as a sensibility based on the fundamental displacement of man, represents what Michel Foucault would specify as a new* epistème.'[13]

Functionalism tied Modern architecture to content and representation, which is why Eisenman, in his editorial 'Post-Functionalism', hopes to redefine it as a pure abstraction akin to those he mentions in the other arts. It is poignant to reflect that 'Post-Functionalism' was offered, at the time, in opposition to my own and Robert Stern's term 'Post-Modernism', for the latter term became accepted as a description for a symbolic architecture and the former was *not* taken up by the abstractionists. However the importance for Eisenman is not in the acceptance of terms, but rather in the radical redefinition of Modernism. Gone are the Enlightenment goals, the utopian vision, the social engagement—indeed the main ideology 'From William Morris to Walter Gropius' (as Nikolaus Pevsner subtitled the Modern Movement). In its place is extreme abstraction, and all the negatively defined presences of *a*tonality, *a*temporality, *dis*placement etc. Through an ingenious transformational act, Eisenman has managed to turn Modernism into nihilism, proving his point by citing Foucault and his *épistème* and excluding, in the process, the canonic set of definers.[14]

Manfredo Tafuri, 're-reading' James Stirling, Aldo Rossi and many other abstractionists of the early 1970s, also attempts to redefine Modernism by showing that its utopian programme is dead. He speaks, once again, of the 'center destroyed', an absolute alienation from the bourgeois and capitalist world for which a degree-zero style is appropriate (because it cannot be appropriated). All that is left to architecture, after the realisation that society cannot be transformed except by a proletariat seizing the means of production, is an absence of expression, a sublimely useless architecture (or Post-*Functional*). The 'empty sacredness' of Rossi's pure, classical abstractions [15] is above any function, context or utopian programme (although it is emphatically 'social', even 'socialist'). The 'law of exclusion',

15 Aldo Rossi, Gallaratese Apartment, Milan, 1969–72. Boullée's 'architecture of shadows', where shadows replaced ornament, was recommended for the cemetery. Rossi also uses it for the living.

the 'syntax of empty signs' are a perfect response to 'L'Architecture dans le boudoir'—an architecture trapped in the boudoir of Modernist comment, pure linguistic speculation, and constructional realism.[15] The Rationalist architects, of which Tafuri writes, are in many cases, however, committed Marxists of another persuasion and do not completely accept the nihilistic interpretation he puts on their work. They speak instead of the 'autonomy' and 'memory' of architecture and thus for them their reductions do not mean an 'arrival at nothing' but rather, like Eisenman's nihilism, they *represent* a very positive something—the archetypes of architectural history.

Akin to Eisenman's autonomous creation machines, the self-generated buildings produced by rules he has chosen to activate, are those of Hiromi Fujii [16]. The critic Hajime Yatsuka has described their Late-Modern, nihilistic context: '*Once the rules of procedure are specified, the result comes forth completely outside the speculation of the architect as an author, no matter how complicated the operation entailed. The architect is himself responsible for laying out the rules and vocabulary, the mesh-work, the white and gray planes, etc. However, apart from the unlikelihood of anyone else coming up with anything resembling Fujii's works, there seems to be, in the status of the "architect" as manipulator, little room for the romantic myth of the demiurge. . . [But] the meaning is in control of the whole thing, to a point where it is safe to say that it converts the whole into a system of symbols representing the parts that make it up.*'[16] Or, as Fujii himself has put it: '*Psychoanalysis overthrew the Cartesian concept of the subject as a lucid intelligence. . . But with increased understanding of the other part of the subject— that is, the unconscious—the myth of integration was exploded. The division of the self into conscious and unconscious destroyed logos and logic since the division of the subject eliminated the integration between the acquired meanings of things*

and their design meanings. But for this very reason, design-imposed meanings are no longer bound to old-fashioned semantic concepts. Consequently, emphasis is no longer placed on the transmission of meaning but on the importance of the right to generate or produce meaning.'[17]

In effect Fujii, like Eisenman, puts his 'mechanism of meaning' in the role of the demiurge, and then gives it free reign. The intention, like that of other Late-Modernists, is to produce something new, totally alien, logical and difficult. '*Art must make perception difficult. . . Metamorphology is one method for the generation of non-conforming relationships. Metamorphology alters acquired meanings (customary codes) for the sake of producing non-conforming relationships.*'[18] He then gives a long list of rhetorical devices—disparity, gapping, opposition, reversal, etc—for achieving difficult perception and altering acquired meanings. At one level this is simply the Romantic and Modernist injunction to 'make it new' in order to heighten perception. But it is taken to a Late-Modern extreme of confusing perception at the literal level, and cutting away familiar codes within which differences and variation might be perceived.

Thus the 'House/Pharmacy', like Eisenman's House X, has windows where they shouldn't be and a flat grid panel on the wall, floor and ceiling—indeed occurring everywhere to break down perceptible transitions [17–20]. Syntactically, exterior facades are rotated into the interior and vice-versa, producing an 'unfinished' exterior, a 'collided' interior and reminders, or cues, of each on both sides. Grids are cut at half points to indicate a conceptual slicing. Black, white and grey heighten the perception of this process. In fact, the *process* is abstracted and, again, represented. Here then is the New Abstraction as representation

11

20

16 Hiromi Fujii, House/Pharmacy, Chofu, Tokyo, 1980. Rule-generated architecture with the architect as the omnipotent rule giver.
17–20 Hiromi Fujii, House/Pharmacy, Chofu, Tokyo, 1980. Interior and exterior are sliced and rotated through each other and marked in such a way, with sliced grids and colour coding, that the operations become visible. The abstraction of surfaces—reduced to blank grids—heightens the perceptions of the abstract rules and the 'estrangement' from familiar meaning.

16
17–19

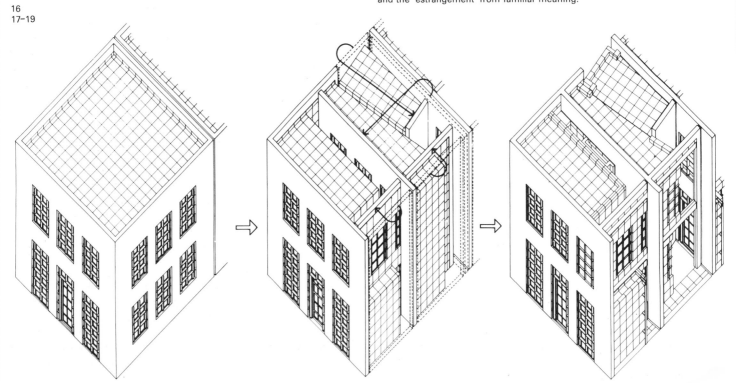

21 Arata Isozaki, Gunma Museum, 1971–74. Isozaki wrote at this time: *'Not only has God disappeared, but we have become incapable of aiming at an interpretation of the universe that all of us can share... I represent this set of circumstances by means of a metaphor of degree zero, or a void at the centre.'* This 'twilight architecture' is abstract and silver-grey, like the grey industrial environment, but lifted to a symbolic and poetic level. (ph Masao Arai)

itself. The ultimate paradox of a meaningless mechanism taken as a goal becoming meaningful, the empty sign becoming symbolic—if understood and manipulated by the architect—is reached.

Both the title and function of the work—'House/Pharmacy'—are ambiguous as is the image. This is a common factor of much Late-Modern work. In Japan in particular the 'Rikyu Gray' of Kisho Kurokawa also seeks an understated ambiguity. By extension, it also shares a correspondence with the abstract reserve of traditional buildings such as Katsura Palace. But these correspondences only add to the absurdity of the overall meaning because recollections are not intended. As Fujii says, the attempt is to induce 'semantic estrangement', not make the user understand the building, as a Post-Modernist would, in its cultural context.

From Mallarmé's to T S Eliot's impersonal author, from the automatic writings of the Surrealists to Nathalie Sauraute's *Tropisms* to the Literature of Silence and Theatre of the Absurd—Sartre, Robbe-Grillet, Burroughs, Ionesco and Beckett—we have had, until recently, a continuously growing tradition of nihilistic writing which has now culminated in a conventional metaphysic of Late-Modernism. Eisenman and Fujii more than other architects, represent the culmination of this tradition, and also of its potential destructiveness. Why build, in a meaningless world—why not destroy? Eisenman would

answer, as we've seen, with the paradox *'one must construct one's deconstructions'*. Citing as ultimate proof of our decentred world nuclear war, the holocaust, today's proliferation of wars beyond human control, he finds metaphysical truth *in the mechanism become autonomous*. Which is more like an Eisenman building—a computer playing chess with itself to mutual checkmate, or the mechanisms of diplomacy, limited war, strategic starvation and international manoeuvering that have taken place recently in Beirut? Whatever mechanisms seem most apt form at a secondary and hermeneutic level the reference for the architecture. Indeed, Eisenman justifies his decentred work in terms of the holocaust, and uncertainty principle, rather the way Alberti and Palladio justified their abstractions in terms of a Christian metaphysic. And we know Eisenman rather admires the formal analysis of Alberti which Wittkower has connected to this symbolism. For these reasons, we might conclude that Eisenman and Fujii are ultimately very religious architects who are always building temples—to an absent God.

A doubt is bound to intrude at this point. What is the relation of the metaphysics to the building task, or the local culture? The idea of designing mass-housing which signifies an ultimate nihilism, or institutional buildings which reflect genocide, will be repugnant to many and illogical to most. Indeed, few clients have commissioned such symbolic work—most of it consists of private houses, except in Japan, where Arata Isozaki and Toyo Ito have been somewhat successful with larger building types. Isozaki, in the Gunma Museum, uses the neutral, grey cube to symbolise, again, the loss of centre, the void where nothing is certain, especially the place of art [21]. The critic Hajime Yatsuka, cited above, discusses recent Japanese work precisely in the context of this nihilism. *'It is the sense of "death" that, according to Isozaki, makes the work of this Viennese architect [Hans Hollein] so exciting, a destructive instinct associated with the memory of the Nazis. There is a connection between these "monumental" affinities and Isozaki's concern for Speer which was already apparent in his project for the Festival Plaza of the World's Fair of 1970, which he called an "invisible monument" inspired by the famous light show of the German architect. . . What is celebrated here is no more than the "form" as an autonomous "signifier". Isozaki was fully conscious of this paradox when he argued, "with the loss of the meanings of celebration the monument turns out to be an altar to this loss".'*[19]

Again we might reiterate that there is everything to be said for architecture as a self-reflexive language and also one symbolic of a metaphysics, so these Late-Modernists cannot be faulted for either their emphasis on system, or their nihilism. The critique, from a Post-Modernist position, concerns the reduction to these two areas alone, and the lack of irony. Other meanings, those of the inhabitants and users, are not incorporated into the message. Before turning to a multivalent approach, we should . examine the counterpart to the elitist nihilism, because this has as strong a pull as any of the beliefs: the New Abstraction, in its beautiful clarity, exerts a compelling hold over the architect's mind.

This term, first suggested to me by O M Ungers with respect to his own work, applies equally well to that of the Neo-Rationalists—La Tendenza—and to several other classical-vernacular architects such as Giorgio Grassi or Rafael Moneo whom we would rather term 'Neo-Tuscan', for reasons which will become clear shortly. In any case, the New Abstraction is positive in its relation to history and local culture, although its solutions are still mediated by a geometrical discipline that keeps them general. In a word, the references are archetypal, not culturally coded.

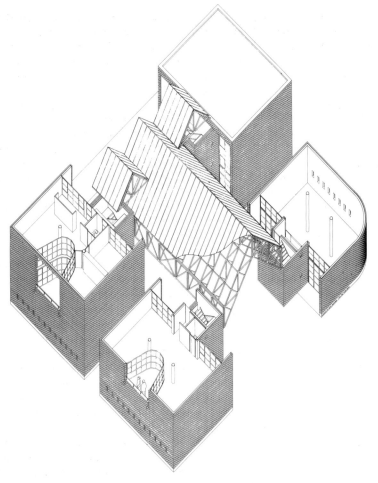

24

22
23

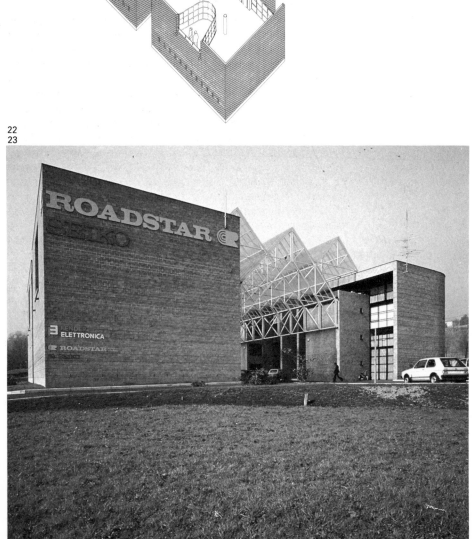

25
26

14

One can see this most clearly in the case of its most mature practitioner, Mario Botta. Deriving his abstraction from that of Louis Kahn and Le Corbusier (with whom he worked briefly), Botta pushes monumental archetypes in a more explicitly classical direction than his mentors. Thus his Balerna Craft Centre [22–23] is divided into a four-square problem, with all four functional areas given separate volumes. A Palladian articulation in plan is crossed with a Kahnian articulation between 'servant and served space'. Thus, four stair cores under four pitched roofs join the four volumes to a central, covered courtyard with giant diffused glazing. Everything is abstracted and conceptualised in its purity. The abstract, square elevations relate to the environment through either a giant window—a black erosion in the brick—or the 12, tiny, vertical slits. Here is the sombre 'architecture of shadows'—Boullée's formula for an ornament of absence. The capitals, mouldings, colour and representational decorations of classicism are also missing, but the building is nonetheless deeply rooted within this Western tradition. Geometry and precisionist detailing more than make up for the missing ornament, an absence which is, no doubt, meant to be experienced positively.

If one were to define the sensibility of this architecture, then, like that of Le Corbusier (another Swiss-born designer), it would have to be termed 'Cistercian'. Le Corbusier, who admired the Abbey Le Tholonet and wrote a panegyric concerned with it (The Architecture of Truth), derived a sensuous pleasure from volumes and functional elements left in their stark essentiality. The contrast of several such elements, in different materials; the reduction of these to a few geometrical forms; and the equation of this with 'truth' appealed to his Swiss, as much as Cistercian, sensibility. For the inheritors of Modernism, this sensibility has remained long after much of the specific ideology had disappeared. Cistercian architecture still appeals to the mind and senses [24]. It combines logical rigour with simplicity and a heavy sensuality. Stones are cut with sharp edges, left rough in the centre to cast shadows, placed on each other following a structural clarity and treated individually as if they were Christian souls to be saved. The love of the saint is combined with that of the schoolteacher. There is much of both behind the New Abstraction. Its patron saint is the ever-complex Adolf Loos, and its scripture his humorous and ironic aphorisms (which tend to be read straightforwardly by the Modernist, with unfortunate results). One of his more sensible formulae was that architecture resides in the monument or grave, 'useless' buildings.

Similarly today's New Abstraction tends to approach the monument and grave in its semantics, and geometrical ornament in its style. Toyokazu Watanabe, like Rossi a writer on Loos, builds noble boxes in single materials that recall Loos' work. Their sole ornament is the emphasis on geometrical figure, voided rectangle and massing [25]. The antecedents are clearly classical and Neo-Classical, the Palladian ordering and reductive aesthetic not only of Loos, but also of Ledoux.

Demetri Porphyrios has summarised part of this tradition in

22, 23 Mario Botta, Craft Centre, Balerna, 1977–79. Platonic volume and structure abstracted and given maximum rhetorical contrast through the tropes of simplicity, reduction, homogeneity and juxtaposition.
24 Cistercian Abbey of Silvacane, Provence, France, 1175–1230. Ultimate spiritual concentration in architecture, the expression of extreme reduction and constructional logic. Each stone is treated as a work of art, and Christian soul. (ph Jencks)
25 Toyokazu Watanabe, Sugiyama House, Osaka, 1980. Ziggurat massing and classical axes in a minimalist architecture of concrete and void, takes up the Loosian theme of the monument and the grave. (ph Hitoshi Kawamoto)
26 Miguel Garay, Casa Mendiola, Andoian, Spain, 1977–78. The New Tuscanism of Spain and Italy uses classical composition principles and order without capitals, triglyphs or other Doric parts. The minimalist order has, however, shed its Tuscan crudeness and become quite elegant and aristocratic.

his 'Classicism is not a Style' (Architectural Design 52 5/6). This title with its Loosian paradox invites the rejoinder: 'Indeed classicism is not a style, but all the examples collected in this volume have the same one'. It is the 'New Tuscanism', because of its delicate chastity. The contemporary work of Miguel Garay, José-Ignacio Linazasoro, Giorgio Grassi, Leon Krier, Aldo Rossi, and the past work of the Swedish classicists such as Gunnar Asplund, or Germans such as Heinrich Tessenow—all work which Porphyrios terms 'Doric'—is really Tuscan because of its severe order [26]. The columns are never allowed to have Doric fluting, and as in the Tuscan Order there is only a blank frieze. Indeed, like the Neue Sachlichkeit with which it has affinities, it never allows an explicit Doric capital.

Porphyrios has defined the ideology of this approach as against what he terms 'Modern Eclecticism'—'the late work of Gropius and Wright . . . the mature work of Aalto . . . the early work of Venturi, Moore and Graves'.[20] Launching an attack on the pluralism and 'indiscriminate toleration (sic)' of Post-Modernists, he arrives, as we might guess, at 'an urgent plea for closing architectural discourse towards the constructional logic of vernacular and its mimetic elaboration: classicism'.[21] His definition of classicism is itself a simplified version of Neo-Classicism, a reduction on a reduction, on the austerities and prohibitions of a Colen Campbell, or Abbé Laugier.

Against the vast outpouring of industrial kitsch which he finds everywhere and sees Post-Modernists everywhere as promoting, he sets an exclusivist monotheme: the representation of 'constructional a prioris'— e g 'load-bearing' versus 'load-borne' elements, or column versus lintel. The idea is to turn such constructional necessities into 'myth', much as did the classical temple. That the 'mythopoeic' transformation of construction was also attempted by Mies, the Constructivists and countless nineteenth-century builders such as Paxton is conveniently overlooked by Porphyrios as he 'closes the architectural discourse' down to Ancient Greece, and the vernacular—'entasis, architrave, the Order'. Not even the Roman dome is permitted, such are the insidious dangers of pluralist kitsch!

It is clear that in his writings, at any rate, Porphyrios is determined to be one of those terribles simplificateurs that has operated in politics since the French Revolution and in art politics, as E H Gombrich has pointed out, since Early Modernism.[22] As in a good advertisement, the doctrines of such polemicists are easier to understand if reality is made terribly simple. The problem is, however, that the tradition of classicism has not been heretofore reduced to constructional representation; its 'mythopoeic power' has always had a much wider reach into society, spiritual goals and all the non-constructional content that people find compelling. If Porphyrios and Frampton, among others, find this content 'kitsch' then it may reflect not only on themselves, but also the content of an agnostic, consumer society. One doesn't have to agree with their taboos to understand their genesis.

However dubious it may be philosophically, it is still true that oversimplification may produce beauty, especially when it is practised with conviction. And if the New Tuscanism is slightly ridiculous as dogma, it is still very sensible as art. Its practice may not make kitsch disappear, but its existence is important as offering a further choice. That is for the pluralist. For dogma reified into an homogeneous Tuscan style offers greater possibilities for opposition to other equally valid approaches, and when these are collected as a totality and conceived of as a system, they can again generate meaning, as the Five Orders did, by being juxtaposed. This reincorporation of an ideology as a style is necessary for the development of various genres, indeed for the very notion of genre, because it allows a freedom of choice and comparison among alternatives. No doubt ideologues will deplore this fact. And one can well imagine that the Ionic and Doric modes were also conceived of as exclusive systems. And that comedy, tragedy and pastoral—obvious genres—had purist defenders who laid down the rules for strict observance: the unities of time, place, mood and the internal consistencies of plot and language. But the knowledge of their mutual opposition increased their potency, first in the Roman age [27] and then in the Renaissance so that like the Orders they formed a system of differences. It is a mark of maturity, both philosophical and emotional, to be able to accept competing systems of expression while still mastering their transformation and mutual opposition.

The New Tuscanism would not appear half so interesting without its potential opponent, the 'New Corinthian' (the work of Moore, Venturi, Portoghesi), just as Doric power gains its strength by opposition with Ionic grace. The debate in architecture is often reduced to a diatribe between equally valid sensibilities and states of being conceived by their exponents as exclusive and totalistic. Such are the recent defenses of Modernism offered by Aldo van Eyck, Martin Pawley and Berthold Lubetkin.[23] The defense of the faith in Modernism becomes harder and harder to follow today as the ideology fractures into

many parts, and leaders, when they do lead, command groupuscules. It may well be that the above-mentioned three, as so many other Late-Modernists, have only in common a mutual aversion to Post-Modernism.

The work and doctrine of O M Ungers, however, is very positive in what it stands for: the New Abstraction as signifying architectural *themes*. He puts forward the autonomy and self-representation of architecture in *Architecture as Theme*: '*An architecture that does not derive its themes from itself is like a painting that tries to be nothing more than a photographic reproduction. The theme and the content of architecture can only be architecture itself.*'[24] One can spot the paralogic—by rights he should state that painting also must 'derive its themes from itself'—and yet recognise this half-truth as an important position, especially in the art world today. No doubt all art is, in part, *about* previous art in the very important sense that its traditions and conventionalised themes come from the past. But it is also partly about something else, as architecture can be, the very thing Ungers derides; and he dismisses this because in our epoch this content is so often sentimentalised, or commercialised.

Ungers then compares architecture with the other abstract art that is often advanced in such debates—music—and continues by defining his notion of theme: '*Once a theme has been identified, it may undergo variations and be transformed at will, yet it is fundamental that there should always be a theme as a basis for the project. . . This is the really creative, conceptual act that must be carried out in designing. In the same way as the working hypothesis determines the direction of thought in scientific research, the theme defines ideation, content and artistic expression in architecture.*'[25] What does Ungers understand by a theme? On the one hand 'fantasy and ideas'—for instance his college in the shape of a ship at the mouth of the Weser River [28]. On the other hand, 'the house as a . . . wall . . . courtyard . . . box . . . egg'—for instance his Berlin housing illustrated in this issue. The theme is then really a Neo-Platonic *concetto*, a driving idea behind design, which Ungers seeks to *transform* through all the parts and the whole, so that, like a symphonic theme, it is varied while still remaining recognisable. This, the oldest of architectural ideas, produces a pleasing unity with variety, and the thing which distinguishes it from previous theories is that Ungers wishes to keep it abstract and tied to the architectural language alone. 'Architecture about architecture', the slogan of the Rationalists and Eisenman in the 1970s, is subtly transformed to 'architecture about architectural themes'. His New Abstraction generalises the thematic parts—stairways, windows, doors—in their diagrammatic neutrality, a practice not far from that of Le Corbusier. But then he juxtaposes these idealised themes, even from different periods, in a picturesque, transformational way so that they become heterogeneous—and this is the opposite of Le Corbusier's Purism. In a sense, the New Abstraction is just Modernism using all the archetypes of history, but informally.

27

27 Cubiculum Boscoreale, 40–30 BC. The representation of three genres—from left to right pastoral, tragic and comic—had been standardised by the time this villa was completed and Vitruvius wrote about the convention. The three genres, five orders and such semantically coded conventions as rustication gave the classical architect a rich palette of meaning. (The Metropolitan Museum of Art)
28 O M Ungers, Institute of Navigation, Bremerhaven, 1979, under construction 1982– . '*The image of a ship was an evident idea that resulted both from the functional programme and from the site.*' The institute is to train navigators, and is on a river port.
28

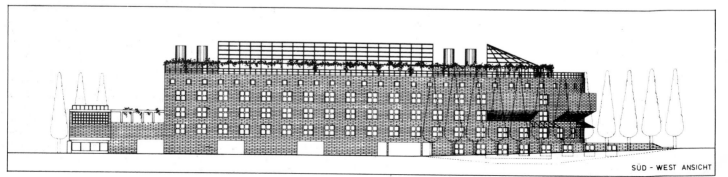

SÜD - WEST ANSICHT

The New Representation

If the Abstractionists regard all non-architectural content as corrupt, kitsch, ephemeral, irrelevant or simply trivial, they are not alone in doing so: in commercial society all significant content is tainted in varying degrees by its marketing, and everyone suffers this contamination with varying degrees of consciousness and sadness. Religion, death, sex, power, love—the heavy themes of civilisation—or affection, sport, food, games—the light ones—are increasingly tainted by Ersatz the more successful they become, and this is true even of authentic creations, or individuals. This fact has led many critics, such as Kenneth Frampton, to despair and absurd comparisons: *'From an ideological point of view, today's Realist avant-garde [Post-Modernism] serves to mask the cultural and political bankruptcy of late capitalism. One could argue that "fluorescent" Post-Modernism plays a role in respect of welfare state consumerist culture close to that played by* Heimatstil *kitsch in the Third Reich.'*[26] Venturi and Moore, according to this reading, are either unwitting tools of a soulless late capitalism, or lackeys of power like Albert Speer.

This ridiculous notion is obviously brought on by an advanced case of that intellectually debilitating sickness 'kitsch consumption' and we might excuse such mental lapses because of the virulence of the disease. It has affected everyone, as I said, and caused certain critics and militants—Vidler, Eisenman, Porphyrios, Gregotti, Zevi, Leon Krier—to lose their sense of perspective. When discussing such Post-Modernists as Venturi, they are unable to distinguish the use of kitsch elements from the kitsch use of elements, Pop from pop and, presumably, a Lichtenstein from a billboard.

Frankly, it's obvious their confusion is feigned, and intended for polemical reasons; they intend to smear Post-Modernists with the tarbrush of kitsch and then move back to the heroic stance of the Modernists–that is elevating public taste to an industrial vernacular, or 'critical regionalism' (Frampton's as yet undefined approach). Opposed to this, the 'Realists' of Post-Modernism wish to engage the existing language of a culture, on all its levels including the vulgate, in order to send it non-kitsch messages. The growth of this tradition stems from Italian and German semiotic work done in the late 1950s, and the theoretical work on popular culture done by the Independent Group, and Marshall McLuhan, in the early 1960s.[27] This developed, in an architectural context, in many directions including *Meaning in Architecture* (Jencks and Baird, 1969) with its emphasis on symbolism and pluralism and *Learning from Las Vegas* (Venturi, Scott Brown, Izenour, 1972) with its emphasis on differing, popular taste cultures.

Robert Venturi has become the architectural spokesman for symbolism, and recently he has refined his views on representation to focus on appliquéd ornament: *'In the progression of our ideas about appliqué, first as spatial layerings, then signboard, and then ornament, we came to appliqué as representation in architecture. . . Manifestations of this approach to symbolism in architecture are essentially two-dimensional and pictorial. . . In our time, economy and industrial standardization on the one hand and lack of craftsmanship on the other justify this simplified, repetitive and depictive approach to ornament.'*[28] We can see their simplified ornament in Pop versions of wall paper or traditional classical motifs, local codes which they distort in Princeton or Iraq, [**29a,b**] or their 'over-all pattern' ornament, the Best Products Showroom which is a decorated shed with giant flowers stencilled all over the porcelain panels. Venturi justifies this *near–* kitsch appliqué, its prettiness and lack of craft, by a version of the Realist argument: industrial society can't afford expensive materials or real craftsmen and

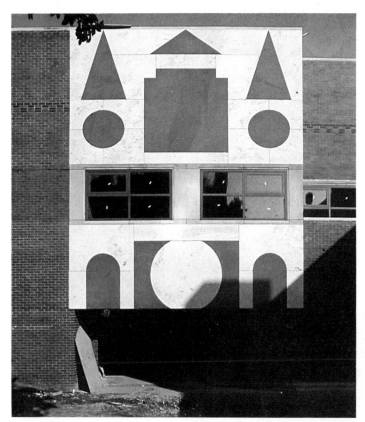

29(a) Venturi, Rauch and Scott-Brown, *Gordon Wu Dining Hall*, Princeton, New Jersey, 1981–3. Symbolic ornament is treated as flat appliqué which indicates at once its flat planar quality – in keeping with the ribbon window and Modernist construction – and application: the patterns press up to the edges of the white background. The Serlian ABA motif, often a sign of doorway or entry, has a rather Early Renaissance feel to it, and resembles an implicit face. (ph Venturi, Rauch and Scott Brown)

29 (b) Venturi, Rauch and Scott-Brown, *Commercial and Residential Buildings*, Khulafa Street Development, Amanat Al Assima of Baghdad for the Ministry of Awqaf and Religious Affairs, Iraq. The architects have used fragments of an 'over-all pattern' on a Modernist ribbon window construction. Here again ornament is symbolic, stylised Moslem signs, which are rendered with a generic simplicity. Like blown-up wallpaper patterns they announce their insubstantial, generic nature as against the craftsman's patient care. Whether this is perceived as pastiche, or as a sensitive reinterpretation of tradition will obviously depend on the final detailing and construction.

has to perceive its signs quickly from a moving car.[29]

Of course, the results of this are not real kitsch, however much Frampton *et al* wish they were, and one can see the 'critical resistance' of Venturi to a commercial society, just as much as that society's resistance to Venturi's irony. If anything, Venturi is producing just the kind of 'critical regionalism' for which Frampton is calling, because he is using local codes in a critical and resistant way, even in an 'ordinary and ugly' way.

The more youthful followers of Venturi, some of whom are collected in this issue, continue his tradition of ironic *and* affirmative realism. Robert Stern represents the pleasures and moods of ritual bathing; ACE represents local, California building types; Stanley Tigerman, in his Anti-Cruelty Society Building, the double attitudes involved in killing and rehabilitating stray dogs. Helmut Jahn represents the old notion of the corporate cathedral, the church of business shooting its beacons of silver light to the heavens, like the Chrysler and Empire State Buildings [**30**].

This representation is a positive step beyond the mute neutralism of Modern architecture. Post-Modernism has made architecture representational once again. But there are several disturbing questions to be asked. As Venturi states: '*I have been concerned with ornament whose content is historical.*'[30] As Paolo Portoghesi and Robert Stern argued at the 1980 Venice Biennale, 'The Presence of the Past' is the *content* of today's architecture. Historicism, 'architecture about previous architecture', is not so very far from the New Abstractionists' position! They both betray the crisis in content which can not be named: society does not provide enough credible public content for which to build, and therefore architects have to fall back on the bank of historical architecture to sustain their credit. In an age when building tasks are not cathedrals but Best Showrooms, the architect is forced, as Stanley Tigerman has begun to understand, to represent black humour. The content of architecture to be represented today may be an *absent* spirituality, and absent public realm, and how can one represent these absences except in partial, ironic and synthetic ways?

Before we engage this question, let us look at one of its conspicuous symptoms, the building which Paul Goldberger called 'Post-Modernism's first monument', that is Philip Johnson's AT&T Building. This is, no doubt, a dignified addition to the Manhattan skyline and a positive change in direction for skyscraper imagery, but in two ways it does betray aspects of kitsch. The entrance *Serliana*, based on the Pazzi Chapel, focuses not on a high altar but on a gilded representation of the goddess of AT&T—a kitsch 'devaluation of symbols' which Sigfried Giedion deplored in Post-Napoleonic architecture. Secondly, since its pink granite appliqué is only a thin curtain wall veneer, and since its real construction, at the base, consists of classical cross-braces, there might have been a relation between symbol and constructional reality, the very stuff of classicism [**31**]. Johnson and Burgee, by not exploiting this oldest of classical ideas, have been unfaithful to the very tradition they support. To say this is not to argue for a constructional literalism, but rather for a selective constructional *symbolism*.

The crisis in representation is thus not only concerned with the lack of credible content, but the lack of a live tradition, one that understands the deeper levels of classicism. In a constructional sense, Mies' representational I-beams at the Seagram Building are closer to the Doric Temple than Johnson's hanging blank wall, but both are only fragmentary symbolic systems. The Parthenon was a full representational system worked out

30 Helmut Jahn, Bank of the South West, Houston, Texas, 1982–. A centralised plan produces, as usual, the Skypricker, inheritor of the Chrysler and Empire State Buildings, with their shafts, beacons, fountains and hyperdermic needles. Floor setbacks, lighting and the top facets accentuate the heavenwards drive. (ph Jahn)

in all its parts and iconography, something that took over two hundred years of slow, piecemeal and conventional development.

We are not about to produce such integrated temples, any more than we are about to start worshipping Athena, but an embarrassing fact is brought out by their presence. As long as these monuments survive, they will remind us of how limited and partial are our attempts at representation, how tentative are the Best Showrooms and AT&Ts, the Cathedrals of Business and the Anti-Cruelty Societies. This depressing conclusion might lead many architects straight back to Modernism, its muteness and agnosticism, because at least these aspects acknowledge a crisis of content. But this is clearly regressive, a reactionary stance which refuses to learn from recent mistakes and face up to the problem of representation in an agnostic age.

The Art of the Public Realm

If architects are to represent anything publicly credible then they must try to define the convivial public realm, the 'space of appearance', in Hannah Arendt's words: *'The term "public" signifies two closely interrelated but not altogether identical phenomena. It means, first, that everything that appears in public can be seen and heard by everybody and has the widest possible publicity. For us, appearance . . . constitutes reality. . . Second, the term "public" signifies the world itself, in so far as it is common to all of us and distinguished from our privately owned place in it. . . The public realm, as the common world, gathers us together and yet prevents our falling over each other, so to speak. What makes mass society so difficult to bear . . . [is] the fact that the world between them has lost its power to gather them together, to relate and separate them.'* [31] In such well-known passages, Arendt defines aspects of the public realm as seen in the permanence of monuments, the artifice of art, the action of statesmen, and the revolutionary events of small democratic groups. We can see, in her many writings,[32] how the public realm must be defined in a multiple way, and this means for architecture three things.

First, it must show the artifice and permanence associated with things that outlast a mortal life. If an individual's death is assured and private, then the significance of his or her life must be transformed to a public level if it is to be remembered. Architecture memorialises, as a public art, and it keeps memories of individuals, social values and ideology. Many architects in the classical tradition have acknowledged this since Vitruvius insisted on the memorialising role, and one can see in the heavily monumental and symbolic work of Ricardo Bofill just this intention of permanence [32]. Triumphal arches of housing, arcades, surround a round *place* given over to the pedestrian, the enclosed urban realm—all of these spaces are convivial public realms which only lack their credible social sanctions (not particularly Bofill's fault, but rather that of an agnostic client).

Second, the public realm has to be established collectively through action—a near-impossibility given the way architecture is produced today. Only very few acts of collective participation—Erskine at Byker, Moore at the Piazza d'Italia—have

31
32

31 Philip Johnson and John Burgee, AT&T Building, New York, 1978, 1980–83. Massive cross-bracing, a traditional Roman motif, will be hidden by the veneer of pink granite; the structure and construction are not symbolised. (ph Jencks)
32 Ricardo Bofill and Taller de Arquitectura, Les Arcades du Lac, St Quentin-en-Yvelines, France, 1975–81. The permanent monument in the round *place* symbolises, in this case, the absence of any credible building, monument, or religious function, in the suburban society. The public realm is nonetheless present and celebrated in the enclosed pedestrian space. Concrete 'Baroque classicism' is being refined further by the Taller. (ph Jencks)

33

34

elicited the creative exchange between social desire and architectural rhetoric, and one is forced to reassert again and again that a small-scaled democratic forum is the precondition for a full architectural poetics.

Third, the public realm must be accessible, understood and enjoyed by the public, and in an architectural language which is partly conventional. And here lies the misunderstanding of those, such as Frampton, who also support the necessity for a *res publica*. For the last ten years Frampton and I (not to mention George Baird, Nicholas Habraken and a host of other architects) have been insisting on a political forum and public realm as the necessary, if not sufficient, condition for a lasting architecture. But after this initial area of philosophical agreement, we part company on the crucial issue of accessibility: Frampton supports a degree-zero architecture of Giorgio Grassi and Aldo Rossi, something that may be highly poetic, but which is essentially esoteric, distanced and sometimes even private. The irony is that of proferring a private architecture as public, something dedicated by The Happy Few to The Unhappy Many! So upset is Frampton by the spectre of kitsch that he condemns all accessible architecture—that of Moore and Bofill—as 'deliquescent'. Thus in a single act of personal taste, the tragic interference of private sensibility with public philosophy, his argument dismisses precisely that tradition which seeks to make contact with a public.

For what is Post-Modern architecture? An architecture which is doubly-coded, part Modern part other, part elite part popular, which engages the difficult task of speaking to a consumer society without loosing its integrity. Charles Moore's Piazza d'Italia, conceived in participation with the Italian community of

New Orleans, was also conceived as a public action to create the public realm—and soon the fountain may indeed engender the supporting growth to surround it. Hollein, Venturi, Graves and Bofill all use the vulgate language *in part*; they use clichés, stereotypes, conventions, hackneyed expressions, but carefully within a creative context and only to make contact with a mass culture. Without that contact there is no public realm and no public architecture in our time.

Abstract Representation

If architecture is *the* public art, the accessible art of daily life where 'appearances are revealed', then it must go beyond the dialectic, or perennial debate, which so occupies the present. We have seen that each position—the New Abstraction and the New Representation—is founded on the irreducible truth, albeit a partial one, that architecture must represent its own themes as well as public, extrinsic themes. Any architect will naturally fall by temperament towards one side or the other for the simple reason that it is hard to be responsive to both obligations at once.

There is also a historical and theoretical reason for this fundamental division. Both approaches lack an articulation of the way architecture conveys its meaning most effectively. Architectural messages are conveyed best when slightly veiled—more implicit than in painting and more explicit than in music. Totally explicit or iconic architecture, the Face House in the shape of a face, is troublesome partly because it is reductive—becoming simply the icon—and partly because architecture is ubiquitous, ever present, and cannot afford to proclaim a single

35

36

33, 34 Michael Graves, Plocek House, Warren Township, New Jersey, 1978–82. The 'Keystone House' uses several classical motifs in a veiled way. Not only is the keystone absent, voided above the door, but the two giant columns are turned into piers which layer the space like the frame behind it. Base, shaft and capital are also suggested, without being named. (phs Graves)
35 Michael Graves, Portlandia Study, 1980. The 'Port' is symbolised by the trident, 'Land' by the laurel, trade with China by the rock, and dynamism by the angled, flying pose. The pose relates to the Prometheus statue above the ice-skaters at Rockefeller Center in New York.
36 Raymond Kaskey, Portlandia Model, 1982. The suggestion of northern Indians and the 'Little Rock' girl are a bit too obvious in this dynamic, representational work. (ph Jencks)

message, except in the rare case of a socially sanctioned emblem such as a cross. Some of the representational work in this issue is over-explicit, becoming, if not the one-liner or two-liner, a string of deft quotes strung together.

But if the New Representation faces the problem of becoming nothing but the image, then the New Abstraction has a complementary tendency to remain incomprehensible, or unappealing to all but the architecture lover. Abstract Representation, however, deploys a different procedure from either of these. Basically architects such as Hans Hollein and Michael Graves abstract a theme, stylise it to the point of ambiguity, and then repeat it so that it becomes definitely *sensed*. A halo of suggested meanings surrounds the object, tying it in to previous experience—directing it, if not fixing the meaning. For instance, in his Plocek House, Graves uses the conventional idea of paired columns at the entrance, but then turns them into wall piers and ties them formally to the chimney stack 'column', an interior columnar stair and other veiled columns throughout the house [33, 34] In this way, he both recalls the memory of other columns, and yet distances it from the cliché. In short, it is an abstract representation of the column. The same is true of his representation of the earth (through colour), the window and the wall: they recall these archetypes of experience and architecture but in a suggestive way, by being displaced from the norm. A theme will be stated and transformed, according to the same method that Ungers recommends, but it will also be made unfamiliar so that an imaginative effort is required to see its relation to the type.

That Abstract Representation can be taught, and that it has been a method of design since Egyptian times—sometimes

practised, sometimes lost—is obvious from decorative work. Whether referred to as 'stylisation', or 'imitation not copying', or under other rhetorical figures such as 'metamorphosis', the idea has circulated among painters and architects. Yet it has not been formulated for our generation and the result has been an overemphatic expressionism, whether of theme or icon.

Another example of Michael Graves' work brings out this point. His figure and invention for Portlandia, the emblematic woman over the doorway of his Portland Public Service Building, might be contrasted with both the highly representational seal of the city, from which it derives, and the very naturalistic figure which is being sculpted [35, 36]. Graves, in designing Portlandia, wanted a figure which the citizens could identify and take as their own; he accepted, that is, the accessible role of the architectural and sculptural sign. But after studying the existing seal, the figure of a classical goddess holding a trident, he came to an impasse. The mayor, the city librarian, indeed the people of Portland had forgotten her specific meaning, perhaps because her posture and attributes were so stereotyped. Graves thus had to rederive the symbol intuitively, abstract its representational sources through sketching. And after some exploratory, transformational designs which played with potential meanings, it occurred to him that the city seal had very significant and relevant attributes. He then produced his stylised synthesis of these meanings [35]. Here Portlandia flies along at an angle, not the stable classical cliché, but a dynamic expression of action, billowing skirts and outstetched arms. She holds a trident in one hand, emblem of sea, sign of 'Port', while a sheaf of corn, or laurel, is in the other hand, symbol of peace, sign of the corn-belt, the Mid-West or 'Land'. 'Port'—'land'—'ia' billowing away over her Chinese rock is then a compound stylisation of the fact that the citizens of Portland trade between the west and east, Chicago and China, sea and land. She can be seen as a symbol of this because the signs have not become too specific and reductive, and it is of interest that the citizens of Portland responded to this fact.

When Late-Modern architects asked that she be banished from the building, several merchants and laymen lobbied for her return. The people participated in an act that resulted in an architectural and sculptural decision. The controversy continued and finally they got a version of their stylised ribbons back. After that a competition was held for the sculpture, and they made their wishes known on that. The result will be, unfortunately, much more a piece of official, representational art than the Graves' design [36]. It suffers from recalling the 'Little Rock' girl and other well-known formulae. But it is significant that Graves' design was instrumental, like Charles Moore's Piazza d'Italia, in creating the public realm, in forcing *action*, that aspect Arendt defines as essential to the *res publica*. It is also significant as an example of Abstract Representation: it could coalesce the social aspirations of a city in a way that was cre- ative and suggestive, not reductive. It could also bring out the other more implicit anthropomorphic images in the building, the face of the large window, the shoulders of the keystone and the tripartite elevation—feet, torso, head. These images are also abstract, indeed extremely veiled, but nonetheless present.

It is Graves' ability to convey implicit messages through architecture, ornament, sculpture and painting that sets his work above that of his contemporaries. Not only his commitment to art, which others share, but his ability as an exploratory artist is rare. In this he is close to Le Corbusier and closer still to Renaissance architects Raphael and Michelangelo. Perhaps he will dominate his period as they did theirs, because he also combines the arts in a creative way. Or, more likely, several opposing architects, all of whom can draw creatively, will set opposing standards. In any case, Graves' architectural power also springs as much from his method, as his ability to draw and paint. From abstraction it gains the virtues of generality and suggestion, and from representation the advantages of familiarity and reference. It can refer to existing aspirations while remaining both open and mysterious.

Notes

1 Peter Eisenman, 'Building In Meaning', *Architectural Forum*, July/August 1970, pp 88, 90. '*This collection remains provocative partially because of these flaws, which serve as an initial indication of a larger debate: the still undrawn lines between architecture as an elitist phenomenon, and architecture as a popular social remedy.*' (p 90)

2 Peter Eisenman, 'Real and English: The Destruction of the Box I', *Oppositions* 4, pp 5–34. Eisenman writes '*. . . it must be necessary to fabricate an historical fantasy about Leicester. . .*' (p 7) See also his footnote 6.

3 See Le Corbusier-Saugnier, 'Le Purisme', *L'Esprit Nouveau* 4, Paris 1921, and *Towards a New Architecture*, trans John Rodker, London 1927, pp 22, 96. Saugnier was Amédée Ozenfant's pseudonym.

4 Peter Papademetriou, 'Le Corbusier à la Mode', *Architectural Design*, January 1971, p 24.

5 Peter D Eisenman, 'Meier's Smith House', *Architectural Design*, August 1971, p 524.

6 See 'Special Issue Peter Eisenman', *A+U*, January 1980, pp 25–147.

7 *Ibid*, pp 31 and 33.

8 'A Poetics of a Model: Eisenman's Doubt', in *Idea As Model*, Catalogue 3, IAUS, Rizzoli, New York, 1981, p 121.

9 *Ibid*, p 121.

10 *Ibid*, p 123.

11 *Ibid*, p 123.

12 Many existentialist writings of the 1950s summarise these themes. See for instance Erich Heller, *The Disinherited Mind*, New York, 1957; William Barrett, *Irrational Man*, New York, 1958 and Wylie Sypher, *Loss of the Self in Modern Literature and Art*, New York, 1962.

13 Peter Eisenman, 'Post-Functionalism', *Oppositions* 6, Fall 1976, pp ii–iii.

14 The canonic set of definers of Modern architecture was formulated by historians Giedion, Hitchcock, Zevi, Pevsner and others and later redefined by Benevolo, Banham and Scully. For a comparative list see my *Late-Modern Architecture*, London and New York, 1980, p 32.

15 See Manfredo Tafuri, 'L'Architecture dans le boudoir', *Oppositions* 3, New York, 1974, p 45.

16 Hajime Yatsuka, 'Hiromi Fujii's Vision-Reversing Machine', *Oppositions* 22, Fall, 1980, p 2.

17 Hiromi Fujii, 'Architectural Metamorphology: In Quest of the Mechanism of Meaning', *Oppositions* 22, Fall 1980, pp 14–19.

18 *Ibid*, pp 15 and 17.

19 Hajime Yatsuka, 'Architecture in the Urban Desert; a critical introduction to Japanese Architecture after Modernism', *Oppositions* 23, Winter 1981, p 13.

20 Demetri Porphyrios, 'Classicism Is Not A Style', *Architectural Design* 52 5/6, 1982, p 51.

21 *Ibid*, p 56.

22 See E H Gombrich, *Norm and Form*, Phaidon, London, 1966, p 97. Porphyrios has, in his work, introduced applied ornament and acroteria, which have little to do with the mimetic elaboration of construction. See *British Architecture*, *Architectural Design* Special Profile, 1982, pp 156–58.

23 It is hard to characterise the 'Modernism' of these three, especially as they were such fierce critics of it when it was the reigning approach. Van Eyck locates a cultural Modernism, which he supports, in the 1910s with Cubism, Joyce, and the 'Great Gang'—Einstein, Mondrian, Picasso. In opposition to this, Lubetkin would appear to support a Rationalist, Enlightenment Modernism, perhaps a refurbished 1920s Modernism, while Pawley seems to be supporting the progressivist and poetic use of technology—at least in his articles on Mies. See my 'Post-Modern Architecture—The True Inheritor of Modernism' in *Transactions* 3, RIBA, London 1983.

24 Oswald Mathias Ungers, *Architecture as Theme*, Electa, Milan 1982, p 9.

25 *Ibid*, p 10.

26 Kenneth Frampton, 'Modern Architecture and the Critical Present', *Architectural Design* 7/8, 1982, p 25.

27 The German work took place at Ulm, the Italian research culminated in the writings of Umberto Eco; some of this is mentioned and translated in *Signs, Symbols and Architecture*, edited by Broadbent, Bunt and Jencks, John Wiley, London, New York 1980. For a discussion of the Independent Group see my *Modern Movements in Architecture*, Harmondsworth 1973, pp 270–80.

28 Robert Venturi, 'Diversity, relevance and representation in historicism, or plus ça change. . .', Gropius Lecture at GSD Harvard 1982, reprinted in *Architectural Record*, June 1982, p 116.

29 *Ibid*, p 118. '*In the Best showroom loft, big flowers, bold and pretty, camouflage the inevitable banality of the architectural form and read as a sign across a vast parking lot and speedy highway.*'

30 *Ibid*, p 118.

31 Hannah Arendt, 'The Public Realm: The Common' in *The Human Condition*, Anchor Books, Chicago 1959, pp 45 and 48.

32 Among her other books, see *On Revolution*, The Viking Press, New York 1965, which discusses the formation of small public realms during revolutions: the Rätte, Soviets, communes, USA townships, etc.

NEW
ABSTRACTION

OM Ungers, *Frankfurt Fair Galleria*, finished 1983. Architectural 'themes' abstracted–particularly arch, window, grid and galleria. See pages 43–45.

EISENMAN ROBERTSON

Three Projects, 1980–82

Representational Abstraction

These three projects, for which I have respect, nevertheless give me some disquiet and it is perhaps wise to dispose of the doubts before embarking on a more reasoned assessment, for in this way personal and philosophical issues can be distinguished from a more intrinsic analysis.

Peter Eisenman, in his texts, displays his usual contempt for Post-Modernists' attitudes to the past, which he refers to as nostalgic, or kitsch. Such reductivism has now become standard dogma for Institute spokesmen—Eisenman, Frampton and Vidler—to be repeated like a litany. Systematic incantation may not make insults into the truth, but among believers it can certainly work hypnotically.

Secondly, a loosening of Eisenman's previous tenacity can be seen in these realistic schemes, perhaps indeed as a sign of his new realism. His well-announced transformation as 'P.3' (the 3 is E backwards) heralds his third period as 'the man who wants to build not talk'. This attempt to emulate Mies may be exemplary, but it blunts the purity of his message as he becomes, almost, Post-Modern in his new-found interest in context and local symbolism. The partnership with Robertson, the utilitarian Cummins Building, and the two urban schemes have lessened the theoretical rigour—amounting to fanaticism—that was evident in House X. Pragmatism and realism often lead to a blunting of artistic tenacity, except in the rare case of an architect like Charles Moore who may actually be provoked by them. Certainly Eisenman and Roberston are capable of a sublime and aristocractic architecture, in a way the most pure of our time. CJ

Project for Southern Friedrichstadt, Berlin

premiated entry to the Internationale Bauausstellung (IBA) 1984

Peter Eisenman and Jaquelin Robertson with Christopher Glaister and Thom Hunt, Thomas Loeser, Michelle Andrew and John Leeper

In their text, Eisenman and Robertson invent a paradoxical notion of anti-memory, an oxymoron which has it both ways: it both destroys while acknowledging memory. Their 'artificial excavation' is thus a precise act of idealising a past set of grids, eighteenth-, nineteenth- and twentieth-century street patterns, in such a way as actually to erode past imagery. However, three existing buildings are preserved, and the ideal Mercator Grid is shifted 3.3° to indicate the all-too-real Berlin Wall. So, for those who can read their shift, or 'scar', and learn the point of tartan grids, the forms are local, symbolic and memorialising. One could even call them Post-Modern, except that they are so inscrutably abstract. In their abstract idealism they deny the very references to which they refer. It's rather as if Sir Arthur Evans reconstructed an ideal Palace of Knossus and in the process destroyed the real excavation—an accusation sometimes heard. But the scheme is more subtle than this, because it is supposed to be read as an overall symbol on the meta-level. The opaque abstraction is itself a sign of anti-memory, the peculiar symbol of Berlin's unfortunate predicament, of being suspended in limbo between a past wiped continuously away, and an impossible future as a museum divided against itself.

That few could read this meta-level, the three grids, the scar and opaque facades makes the result decidedly sculptural and Late-Modern; that symbolism was intended, and that it is perfectly relevant makes it Post-Modern. Oscillating then between an elite hermeneutic and a creative reinterpretation, the scale will be tipped, either way, in the final construction. It seems that part of the housing to the north-east will be built, perhaps with the shifts and scars indicated in part. What of the museum, towers and walkways? Morphologically these relate to the urban work of Team X, John Hejduk and to Eisenman's own House El-Even-Odd. Compositionally they follow some notions of 'decomposition' from givens, also conceived since House X (see my introduction). The left-over Ls, or as Eisenman says 'els', can be read as fragments of larger volumes, or as extrusions, just as the facades on Kochstrasse can be read as 'One-Half Buildings'. They seem cut-off in mid-flight, also forming Ls with an endless grid-appliqué.

This then is a representational abstraction which refuses to represent anything to the common man on a direct, conventional level, but hopes to persuade him on a higher and subliminal plane.

The City of Artificial Excavation

History is not continuous. It is made up of stops and starts, of presences and absences. The presences are the times when history is vital, is 'running,' is feeding on itself and deriving its energy from its own momentum. The absences are the times when the propulsive organism is dead, the voids in between one 'run' of history and the next. These are filled by memory. Where history ends, memory begins.

The European city today is a manifestation of such a memory-void. As such it presents a crisis not only of history but of architecture itself. During the period of the Modern Movement, historic city centres became places for plunder. With their demolition during the war, and then with the rebuilding and development that followed after the war, they rapidly began to lose their identity. As a reaction to this failure of modern architecture to understand, enhance, or even conserve the historic centres, a new 'post-modern' attitude came into being: the centres became transformed into fetish objects. In general they were treated in two ways. Either fragments of the old urban structure were preserved like discrete bones or relics in a natural history museum, or the bones were reassembled, the skin and

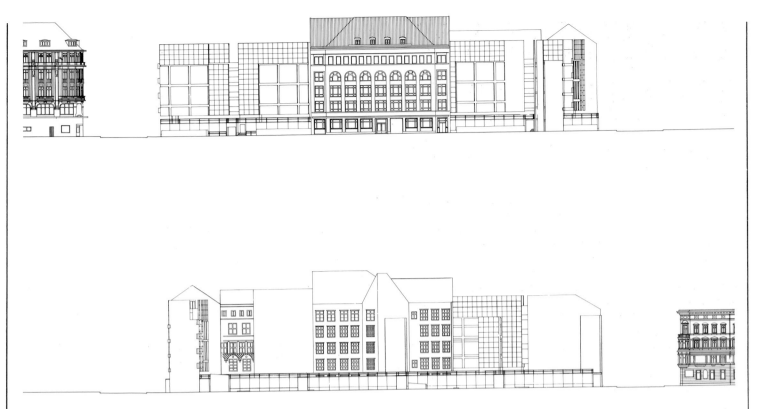

1 Kochstrasse and Zimmerstrasse elevations. The existing building bisects three fragments of the addition. Note the grid L.

2 Plan. The Berlin Wall and the entrance to the garage are to the north; Checkpoint Charlie is to the north-west. The grid shifts acknowledge both the traumatic facts and the garage entrance. Two more rules determined the composition: the tartan grids and the tower Ls.

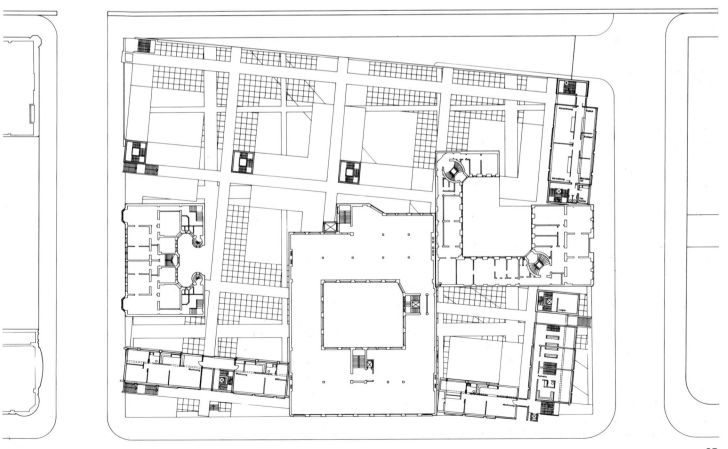

3

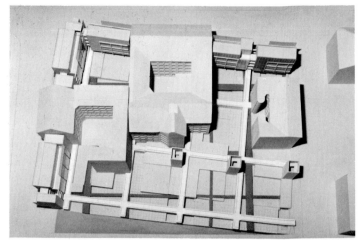

4

3 Perspective showing the walkways, museum tower, old buildings and excavation. The similarity of steps, wall, window and building is obviously meant to confuse the viewer as to what the functions really are. The shifted cross seems to lead to impenetrable walls; the 'scar' on the tower refers only to other scars.
4 Model from the north: the suspension of the scheme midway between excavation and building, real and ideal street grids, finished and unfinished.

flesh restored or hypothetically recreated, and the new assemblage appeared as a kind of stuffed animal, a vignette in a 'natural' setting. The former attitude attempted to freeze or embalm time, the latter to reverse or relive it. In both cases history was reduced to a form of nostalgia, and it reflected an unacknowledged anxiety toward the present. . .

In the conscious act of forgetting, one cannot help but remember.

Our strategy for developing [this] site was twofold. The first intention was to expose the particular history of the site; that is, to render visible its specific memories, to acknowledge that it once was special, was *some place*. The second was to acknowledge that Berlin today belongs to the world in the largest sense, that its specificity and identity have been sacrificed on the altar of modern history, that it is now the crossroads of *every place* and *no place*. In the process of materialising this duality the architecture attempts to erect the structure of both somewhere and nowhere, of here and not here: to memorialise a place and to deny the efficacy of that memory.

This brings us to the concept of anti-memory. Anti-memory is different from sentimental or nostalgic memory since it neither demands nor seeks a past (or for that matter a future). But it is not mere forgetting either, because it uses the act of forgetting, the reduction of the former pattern, to arrive at its own structure or order.

The act of memory obscures the reality of the present, that is, attempts to deny the existence of the Berlin Wall in order to restore the *some place* of the past. Anti-memory on the other hand obscures the reality of the past—the past, which is in fact what renders the reality of the present no place—to create an other place, to create *some place*. Anti-memory does not seek or posit progress, makes no claims to a more perfect future or a new order, predicts nothing. It has nothing to do with historicist allusion or with the values or functions of particular forms; it instead involves *the making of a place that derives its order from the obscuring of its own recollected past.*

In this way memory and anti-memory work oppositely but in

collusion to produce a suspended object, a frozen fragment of no past and no future, a *place*. Let us say it is of its own time.

Our design is highly specific to its site in that it begins from the conditions we found there: three scarred but extant buildings on the site and the Berlin Wall on the north. But proceeding without nostalgia or sentimentality, it eschews patching up, filling in, restoring—which suffocate memory—for another alternative. This alternative, which suggests both presences and absences, which heightens memory in order to enable it to recognise the erasures produced by anti-memory, which depends on the erasures in order to present *itself*, involves both the making and the unmaking of the previous hierarchy. It does this through a process of artificial excavation, superimposition, and substitution. The ground becomes an archaeological site. The most important tool for digging is the Mercator Grid; this becomes the means of access to the archaeological artifact, the implement of anti-memory. A universal geometric pattern without history, place, or specificity, this grid ties Berlin to the world; it is the most neutral and artificial system of marking. This implement serves to etch the plate of memory; it finds and then impresses itself. Through the trace of itself, which in inscribing obliterates, the architecture evolves as a *tabula* of both the actual condition and the artificial one.

Memory is developed, deepened. Working downward, the grid discovers at the lowest level of excavation the trace of the absent wall of the eighteenth century. This invisible wall is plotted on the lowest ground plane as a shadow. Next comes the excavation of the foundation walls of nineteenth-century Berlin—not the actual foundation walls which once existed, but an artificial reconstruction, a hypothetical rationalisation of what they might have been. These walls derive their location from the position of the three existing buildings, which taken together provide the fragments of a former grid. These are then incorporated in a regular and symmetrical pattern on the site: an AABAA bay system in the east/west direction, and an ABABA alternation in the north/south direction. The final B bay at the north is incomplete, to be completed only by reading the Berlin

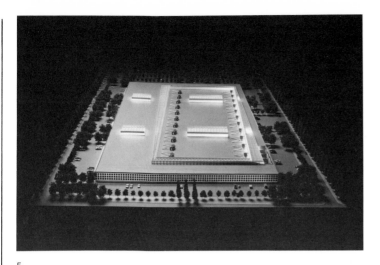

5

5 Cummins Engine Company, Madison, Indiana (under construction). Here again an existing building generates a 'scar' or shift or skylight between itself and the new addition. These consist of four unequal quadrants wrapped by an endless grid reversed in its usual relationship of black to white.
6 Cummins Engine Company, interior perspective.
All photographs by courtesy of the architects.

6

Wall as part of this older grid. This pattern of foundation walls conforms to the regular street grid of Berlin. The walls are made of Berlin brick, and the top of the walls comes up to the present-day ground level of the city. Thus the absent city wall of the eighteenth century, the foundation walls of the nineteenth century, the remnants of the twentieth-century grid as projected upward in the vertical walls of the existing buildings, and finally the Berlin Wall, a monument to the erosion of the unity of the city and the world, form a nexus of walls at different levels which become a composite datum of memory.

Anti-memory is developed. The Mercator Grid superimposes itself as a second set of walls upon and among the historical walls. It is built to 3.3 meters height—the same height as the Berlin Wall. In this way the artificial or 'neutral' walls begin to erase the physical presence of the historical walls. It also renders them inaccessible by causing the ground plane—upon which so much Enlightenment history has been acted out—to become deeply eroded; the ground now becomes a figure of its own history. This ground plane is disconnected both vertically and horizontally from the existing city by canting it 3.3 degrees, creating, this time architecturally, another condition of blockage and division. The horizontal wrenching apart of the site from its surround leaves a permanent scar—a gap between the site and the Wall (this gives access to underground parking). The vertical 'wracking' of the site reveals the old Berlin grid, like an object on the high seas, rising above and below the datum of the city, progressively excavating as it plunges deeper into the ground the sand and ultimately the water upon which Berlin has been built. Because of the canting of the ground plane, the reconstructed grid of the foundation walls forms a series of void containers. . .

Programmatically, the rest of the site is devoted to self-reflections. It becomes a museum of its own archaeology—the archaeology which has been revealed for the first time by the artificial excavation. The museum is entered by crossing the Mercator Walls to a central stairtower, at which point one descends to a large cruciform space occupying one intersection of the Mercator Grid. Three arms of this cruciform are made up of hollow sections of the Grid walls, and allow visual access through peepholes to a series of excavated tableaux—from the eighteenth-century city wall to the restored graffiti of the twentieth-century Berlin Wall. The fourth arm is open and permits one to walk into and onto the actual excavation itself. In this way, the site of artificial excavation becomes the museum's only exhibit. . .

Through superimposition and erasure [the architecture of the Mercator Grid] reveals the double nature of memory and anti-memory; the fragments become a whole as the whole becomes fragment. Time is collapsed into a non-directional movement in which the three isolated core towers become the sign of this stasis. Are these towers in the process of growing or disappearing? The architecture does not predict this; additions and subtractions, further erasures of memory in which the new project itself becomes a fragment of history, could ensue. The architecture admits of these possibilities without preconceiving them. But the object designed for this space neither progresses nor looks back; it is suspended in the present archaeological moment.

For the entire text from which this extract is taken, see AD 1/2, 1983, pp 91–93.

Beverly Hills Civic Center Competition, California, 1982

Peter Eisenman and Jaquelin Robertson

This entry for a competition won by Charles Moore and UIG creates an understated set of piazzas on cross axes—one for the pedestrian and car, the other for the library court—with no visual allusion to the existing Spanish Baroque City Hall of 1932. This understatement would have a heroic, aristocratic calm were it not for the rather banal, concrete detailing and the notional way the cultural complex is 'plopped' down at an angle of 45°. Surely the way this diagonal axis fails to translate across the site in any important syntactic way (the floor patterns and fire station diagonals are token) shows a slackening in tension from Eisenman's House III.

Of interest is the basic dualism of garden versus built-up area. The overlapping city functions and agreeable incorporation of the car—as in Rodeo Drive next door—is very Jane Jacobs and very pleasant. In their text, the architects refer to the 'exhausted language of classicism', but in spite of their protestations one can see its primitivist rebirth in the stereometry of the blocks, the four-sided pavilions and the concrete pergolas down Rexford Drive. The 'totemic objects' also mentioned are not quite the modern totem poles they intend since they lack overstatement and they mark relatively obscure social symbols. This shift to Post-Modern intentions is, however, significant in Eisenman's if not Robertson's work, and to be applauded. At the time of this entry Eisenman told me that he was becoming a Post-Modernist; a month later he was reported in the London Observer as having dropped the style. Is this his only flirtation with the movement?   CJ

1 Landscape and Language

We began from a double proposition: the city of Beverly Hills and the programme of a civic centre. The city of Beverly Hills appears as a landscaped garden in the middle of twentieth-century urbanism, surrounded by the sprawling metropolis of Los Angeles. On the other hand, a civic centre is a type of architectural programme that aspires to be urban: it expresses itself in an architectural language that speaks of a community's cultural identity and public functions. Our project for the Beverly Hills Civic Center proposes an architectural synthesis for this double proposition using the elements of naturalistic landscape and abstract language. Together these two elements create a set of objects and signs in which the resident of Beverly Hills can discover the meaning and mythos of his public life as a citizen. As the historic cities and towns of Europe create an image of a culture through the classical language of architecture and the domesticated landscape of nature, we have tried here to find an equivalent twentieth-century American expression without resorting to a mannered set of kitsch images or a romantic nostalgia for a past that can never be authentically replicated. The given programme was taken as a set of functional, institutional, and symbolic requirements. We have envisioned a realistic image for the Civic Center in which the naturalistic landscape of one side of the site finds its counterpoint and reflection in the language of urban architecture on the other side. Thus the city hall and fire station sites become a continuous natural landscape garden while the site opposite becomes an urban landscape of formal courts and public squares.

2 The Symbolic Gate

We began to define the overall site by observing that the residential north part of Beverly Hills is clearly defined by the garden strip that runs along the northern edge of Santa Monica Boulevard. This strip acts as a symbolic entry as one approaches from the south. It signals a difference between the commercial area and the residential area to the north. Even the flow and pattern of the streets change above this green edge. On the other hand, the commercial area has no comparable definition when approached from the north. We therefore decided to give the Civic Center a strong north edge which would function as a symbolic gate to the urban complex lying behind it. Taking our double cue from the new garden landscape around city hall and the abstract, machine-defined space on the other side of Rexford Drive, we planted a double row of palm trees along Santa Monica Boulevard and the western edge of Rexford Drive and constructed an arcade with columns ('man-made trees', so to speak) on the north-east edge and the eastern side of the street. Rexford Drive itself becomes transformed into a new urban place.

3 The Street: the New American Automobile Plaza

We next addressed the problem of Rexford Drive itself. Since the components of the Civic Center would be organised on both sides of the street, we felt that for practical reasons the present thoroughfare should not be closed and the existing pattern of vehicular movement should not be interrupted. Since the car is the primary mode of transport in Beverly Hills, we wanted the street to be the centre of the civic area—an automobile plaza where functions overlap rather than divide, and where the coincidence of the natural and abstract order is knitted together. To create a unique type of street plaza, we narrowed the north and south entries and widened the drive itself, with a green-covered man-made arcade on one side and a natural arcade of palm trees on the other. Rexford Drive would become a California-style version of the traditional European plaza—both a place and ceremonial route for cars and people. This street/place is further defined by horizontal bands of coloured paving tiles connecting columns and trees, and a diagonal banding of other coloured paving which brings the diagonal grid of Burton Way and the courthouse into Rexford Drive.

4 The Proper Relationship of Institutions: The City Hall/Library Axis

City plans are a cultural record of a city's intentions. They are more than a pragmatic collection of budgets, schedules, and interest groups. A society can express its aspirations and values through the architectural language proposed by the relationship of its institutions. As such, competitions like this one provide an opportunity to propose new ideas which can and should change old systems of priorities. For this reason we strongly rejected the negative symbolism implicit in any decision to place either the new police station or the new fire station on an axis with the existing city hall. Rather it appears to make better institutional sense to put the police station next to the courthouse at the south end of the site, thereby tying the design area to the surrounding impact area in a very real way. This allows the library to be located on axis with the city hall where it makes better symbolic sense. Equally, the present library is too small for its function and does not make a large enough 'footprint' on the ground level.

This reasoning meant a departure from the existing disposition of functions and development priorities as stated in the programme. But upon examination, what initially seemed to be a radical departure turned out to be plain common sense in light of the improved institutional and symbolic relationships set into place. Beyond the satisfaction of achieving the correct symbolic relationships, the relocation of the library into a new building has allowed for the design of a new facility with more than two thirds as much space on one level and interior reading courts for the different divisions. The city hall/library axis becomes a public pedestrian court which enlivens the outdoor area and promotes a dynamic spatial confrontation between the picturesque older city hall and the abstract vocabulary of the new library. This public court and the steps to the roof of the library provide an ideal space for outdoor concerts and a whole variety of civic and cultural events. On the north side of the public court is the community centre with performing arts facilities, exhibition spaces and meeting rooms that complement symbolically and functionally the new library.

5 The Proper Relationship of Institutions: The Police Station/ Courthouse Axis

Once the library and community centre have been located on the city hall axis then the two southern quadrants of the Civic Center can take on the protective and corrective civic functions of the programme. On the site of the present library will be the new police station. The existing building will be renovated and enlarged to accommodate its new functions. South of the new police station is Courthouse Square, which creates a symbolic and axial connection to the existing courthouse. Under the Courthouse Square is the new jail. In this way, courthouse, jail, and police station are linked to one another in a functional and architecturally significant relationship. We have located the new fire station on the site of the old one, a portion of the new station being covered by the natural landscape garden on the west side of Rexford Drive. The cross-axial relationship of the fire and police departments signals their parallel mission in the civic structure.

6 Totemic Object and Other Special Places

Landscaping and language both represent types of human intervention into the order of nature. Landscaping was a means to tame, or recreate at a more manageable scale, that which was beyond man's control. Language was an imposition of an abstract system of communication upon sense experience. In the twentieth century, these origins have been forgotten: landscaping has lost its traditional mythic and symbolic connotations, and the exhausted language of classicism has reduced sense and object meanings to a set of relativistic relationships between signs. This reduction of landscape and language has prevented signs from acting as real objects and real objects from acting as signs. This has resulted in a loss of the totemic object—a sacred, mythical, or archetypal sign which traditionally carried the deepest significance of a culture. The American Indian Village had a totem pole in its centre, and nearly all places that bear the imprint of a culture possess these special symbolic objects that are like coded messages of their history and myths. These often isolated or fragmentary objects, relating only to themselves and their own history, often emerge unexpectedly within an otherwise rational structure of landscape and language. We have attempted to erect a few such 'totems' within the overall site plan for the Civic Center: an empty fragment of a prison tower, a series of traces on the ground plane of the Courthouse Square—of the prison beneath it; the fire station tower which on the interior is a relic of the earlier structure, but outside it is encased in a new shell functioning as a drying tower; the handsome facade of the old fire station has been preserved as an entry to the new one, but moved to a new location and left as a free-standing plane; the brief introduction of the traditional red tile roof in the library square; and the celebration of the ultimate totem—the American automobile in Rexford Drive. Thus, landscaping, supposedly the most 'natural' of man-made creations, and language, the most artificial, here are no longer poles of man's creation, but rather become together part of a new natural order of things. They do so in the same spirit of optimism and enthusiasm with which the existing city hall was built and which now seems to offer another opportunity to achieve these goals of civic life.

1 Aerial view of the model from the east showing the library court and steps focusing on the city hall court. A virtual tension is set up between the two.

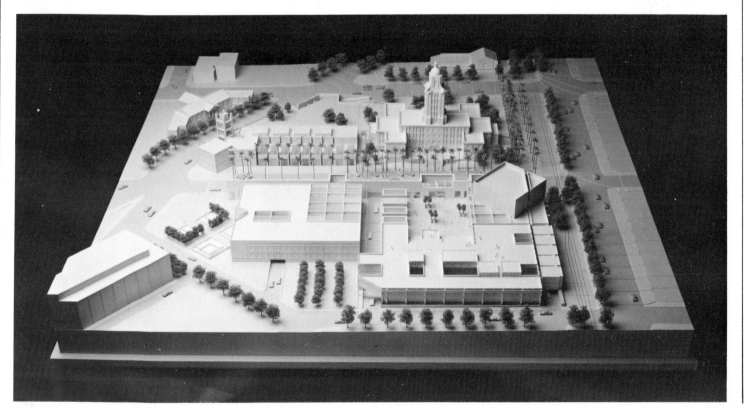

The City of Beverly Hills Civic Center
Beverly Hills, California

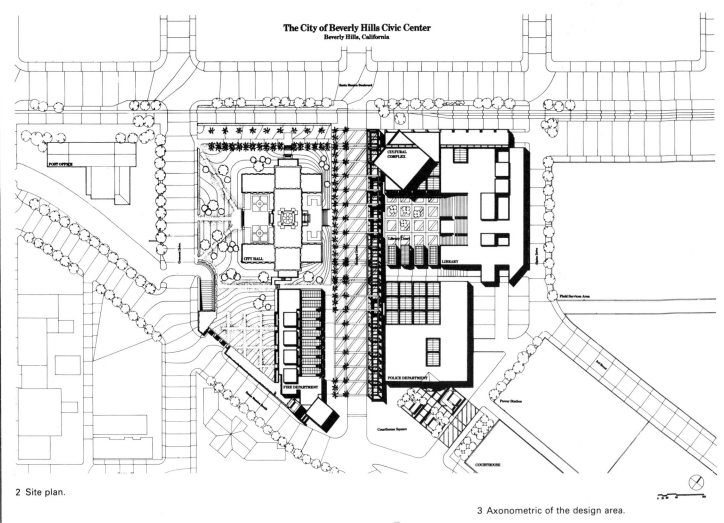

POST OFFICE

CULTURAL COMPLEX

Santa Monica Boulevard

Library Court

LIBRARY

Crescent Drive

CITY HALL

Rodeo Drive

Field Services Area

FIRE DEPARTMENT

POLICE DEPARTMENT

Power Station

Courthouse Square

COURTHOUSE

2 Site plan.

3 Axonometric of the design area.

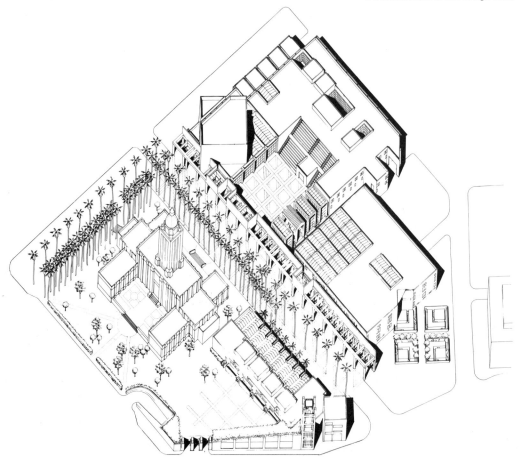

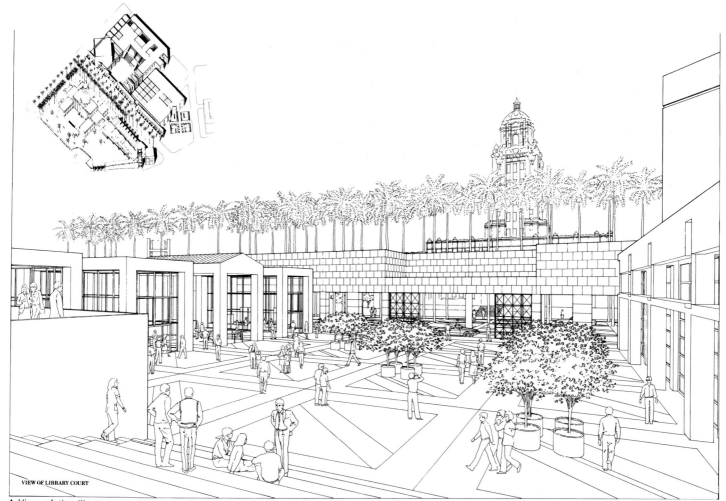

VIEW OF LIBRARY COURT

4 View of the library court, steps, pavilions and stereometry—all primitivist classical.
5 View of Rexford Drive with the concrete pergola shading a mixture of cars and pedestrians; the piers and columns are rudimentary.

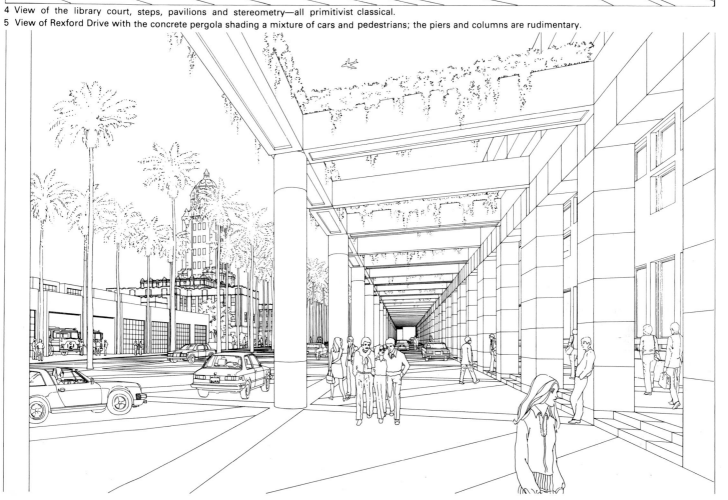

JOSEF WIEDEMANN

Remodelling of the Glyptothek, Munich, 1967–72

Primitivist Classicism

This museum of sculpture was one of the first of its kind in Europe and today, as remodelled after the bomb damage of the Second World War, it has emerged as one of the best. Perhaps no museum sustains such a grave, yet not depressing, mood with such assurety. Moving through the high, vaulted halls, each slightly different but all sharing a common brick structure, one becomes hypersensitive to the white, classical sculpture, which culminates with the Aegina marbles, particularly the pediment group that one can walk up to and touch. These archaic yet simple bodies feel completely contemporary and indeed the Roman vaults are also made to feel both modern and ancient Greek. Wiedemann, in his remodelling of Klenze's masterpiece, has come close to defining the Doric spirit: severe rather than sombre, light and fluted rather than heavy and undecorated as it is often misconstrued today. This can be seen, explicitly, in the L-channel steel beams which hold up an Aegina capital, or implicitly in the regularisation of the coffered brick vaults.

Originally, these had been coloured by Klenze and Peter Cornelius with an effete Raphaelesque decoration. Given the realities of modern craftsmanship and economics, Wiedemann decided to expose the underlying brick forms and give them a unifying wash. Through this transformation the tectonics have become, finally, apparent: Klenze the designer of revivalist stage sets is improved and turned into a primitivist. This transformation was achieved by, it seems, a straightforward approach to precedent, by following the classical language back to its roots, rediscovering the archetype under the décor. Some might fault this creative archaeology for its implicit conservatism, or boredom; and yet the dramatic sequence of spaces around the square courtyard is full of surprise. This is achieved partly by the grouping and lighting of the excellent sculpture. One culminating point, for instance, is the long hall filled with Roman busts placed on simple masonry pedestals—a crowd of senators conversing in a Roman bath.

The Glyptothek was originally conceived by the Crown Prince of Bavaria, Ludwig I, as a centrepiece for his rebuilding of Munich. He intended his new city to become such an 'honour to Germany that no traveller would leave without having seen Munich.' Wishing to commission the 'best architects' available

1 Leo von Klenze, Glyptothek, plan, 1815, shows double row of Ionic columns leading to a domed entrance hall which looks onto the square garden, laid out in the Italian manner. A near symmetry of rooms is achieved. There are full rotundas at both ends of the entrance wing.
2 Josef Wiedemann, remodelled plan, 1968. Rooms are opened up to the court, and paved in stone which underlines slight formal differences. The restaurant (top) provides access to the circular paved courtyard, where seats are also provided.
3 The Roman Room after bombing, 1944. Only a few of the decorative elements remain. The exterior walls were standing, but the vaults throughout most of the building had collapsed.
4 The courtyard with its lunette windows extended to the ground gives each room light and a view, as well as allowing an orientation not previously found. The restaurant gives out onto the court, a welcome refreshment after the Aegina marbles. (ph Rudolf Ehrmann)

1

2

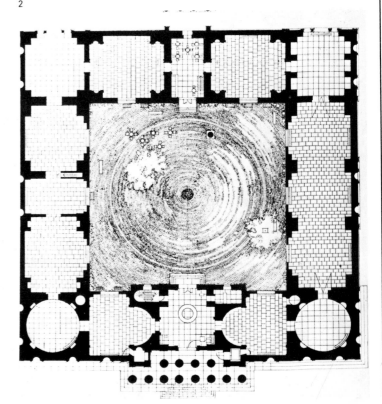

3
4

5

in Europe, he held a competition that was won by Klenze. The building itself was not in the 'purest antique style' that Ludwig had demanded in his initial statements, since it ended up by becoming Ionic rather than his favoured Doric, and eclectically Graeco-Roman-Renaissance rather than Greek. Klenze managed to convince Ludwig in favour of a 'grandiose architectural effect', despite the counter arguments of the sculptor, painter and archaeologist Johann Martin Wagner who proferred a modesty with a 'colour and glitter'. In the event, Munich received a polychromatic interior, which lasted until the Second World War, and has now uncovered the monochromatic austerity and heroic grace that always lay within. It seems like a final victory for Wagner, a triumph of logic and sculpture over architecture;

indeed, it all seems so natural as to be inevitable, as if the classical language itself were speaking. In spite of these feelings, which have aroused those such as Aldo Rossi, the architecture itself is anything but inevitable, or background. It is instead finely tuned to the mood and presence of the sculpture and full of wilful decisions which heighten the archaic.

CJ

5, 6 View through to the rotunda and long hall. The influence of post-war Italians—Scarpa and Albini—is evident in the handling of the masonry background, but the scale is more intense and grand than in Italian remodelled museums. Also, the heroic pendentives of the cathedral of St Front in Périgueux (1120) are recalled, but at a smaller scale. Indeed a slight oxymoronic tension is introduced—large/smallness—by the contrast between the grand style and actual small size. (ph Jencks)

sooner or later to end up in the neighbourhood of kitsch or in esoteric academicism. Equally superficial is the naivité of trying to localise architecture to certain regional or nationalistic conditions. Regionalism in architecture has its climax in a folkloristic architecture and it usually falls back into primitivism, reactionary sentiments and local stupidity.

The New Abstraction in architecture deals with a rational geometry, with clear and regular forms in plan as well as in elevation. In this context, the plan is not the result of a literal interpretation of function and structural conditions but rather of logical, geometrical systems. It is based on proportional relationships and coherent sequences—as was the case in the 'bound system' of medieval architecture, in the Palladian plan, and in Durand's lessons on architecture—rather than on the empirical results of programmes or functional organisation.

The formal language of such an architecture is a rational and intellectual one, not based on accidents or sudden fanciful inspiration. Emotion is controlled by rational thinking, and this is stimulated through intuition. The dialectical process between the two polarities is almost essential in a creative process aimed towards a gradual improvement of ideas, concepts, spaces, elements, and forms. It involves the process of abstraction until the object in its fundamental structure, the concept in its clearest geometry and the theme in its most impressive image appear.

To accomplish this level of clarity, architectural concepts have to be carried through history and seen not as isolated events, as spontaneous inspirations, as clever tricks or as a 'menu of specialities', but as something which does not change at all, which is permanent, and which only proceeds through continuous stages of transformation. The New Abstraction means exactly that: the transformation of ideas and concepts in the course of history. A more precise New Abstraction in architecture will revive basic concepts of space which have occurred in all historical periods: for instance the four-column space, the concept of walls, the courtyard block, the gate, the cruciform building, the square, the circle, the cylinder, the pyramid and the perfect cube—regular geometric and volumetric forms which as universal orders of abstraction represent a quality of permanence. It is not the differentiation of colour and form, of material and style, that will be of importance and significance, not the abundance of shapes, volumes and spaces, but the restriction and the economy of means. The New Abstraction should be the representation of the essential.

1 Bremerhaven School for Nautical Sciences, perspective, 1982. The building as ship with the balustrade as parapet, chimneys as funnels, roof as bulkhead, walls as planks, etc.

O M UNGERS

Perimeter Block on Schillerstrasse, Berlin, 1978–82

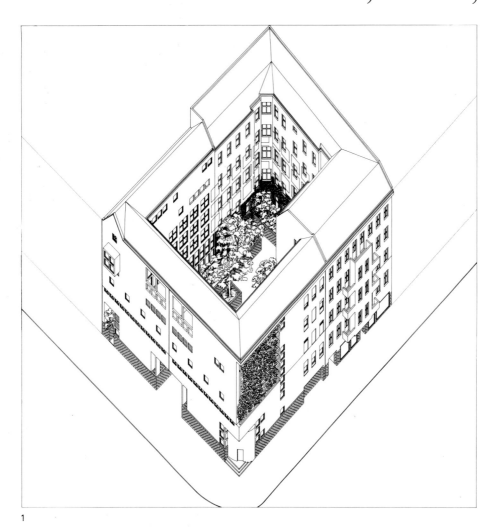

1

Urban transformation and completion

Ungers has transformed and completed the morphology of an existing U-shaped block by ringing the changes on the existing units. Thus a perimeter entity is formed, one of the favoured urban types of the 1970s, in which new and old are merged, not juxtaposed, by a system of differences: related grids, proportional openings, a common brick base and similar painted stucco.

Conceptually, the ordering elements are the quiet interior courtyard (versus the noisy street), the notion of boundary or inhabited wall (a favourite Ungers theme), the abstract fenestration and greenery (not yet grown) and the repetitive, transformed private houses. These amount to self-contained maisonettes forming a mini city palace (Stadtpalais). They have their garden courts, or, on the fourth and fifth floors, garden-courts-in-the-air—in the Corbusian manner. The garden in a house, the house within a large house within a block, are again the themes Ungers often transforms across a single scheme.

Theme and variation, the leitmotif of Ungers' architecture, are

here played stylistically as a picturesque ordering on a white, classical background. Unities, local symmetries, ordered storeys exist in part of each area. Thus reading from the existing housing in Kaiser-Friedrich-Strasse (on the right of the photographs), we find: 1 the theme repeated in a more abstract form with both real and false windows; 2 a vertical row of windows as countertheme; 3 the corner apartment articulated as a full trellis versus (almost) blank wall; 4 the section with open gardens-in-the-air; 5 the enclosed corner apartments with gable. We can see from this that Ungers is using windows as his ordering principle and that the Schillerstrasse facade (on the left of the photographs) is effectively treated as a palazzo with a horizontal layering into storeys. This contrasts with both the Kaiser-Friedrich-Strasse facade and the interior.

In this way Ungers keeps the commonality of the perimeter

1 Isometric projection.
2 Night view, seen from the Kaiser-Friedrich-Strasse. (ph Waltraud Kräse)
3 Day view, seen from Kaiser-Friedrich-Strasse. (ph Ungers)

2
3

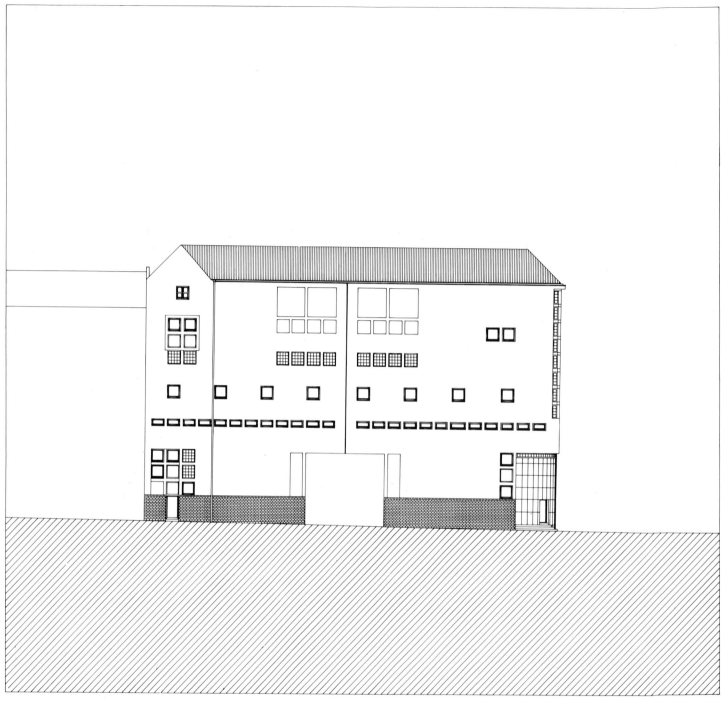

4 Elevation on Kaiser-Friedrich-Strasse.

6-11 Plans, ground floor through sixth floor.

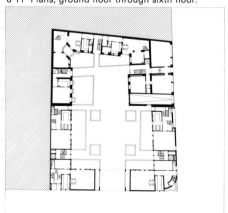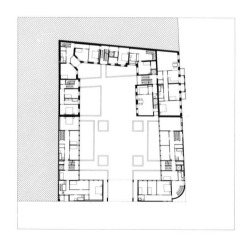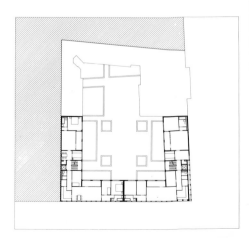

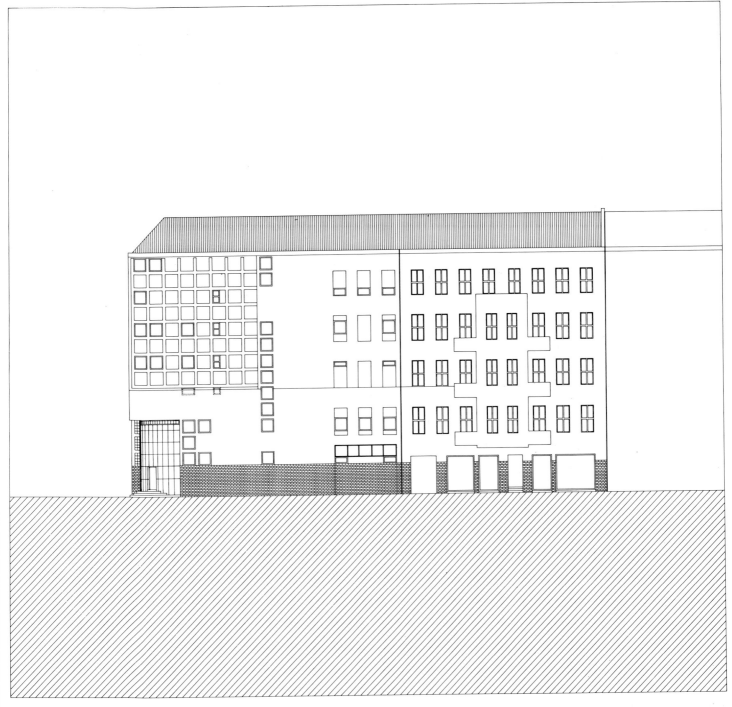

5 Elevation on Schillerstrasse.

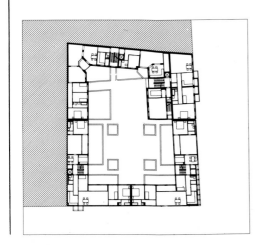
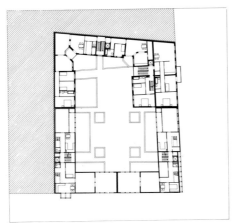
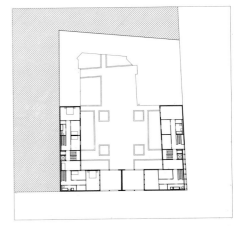

block—making us recognise it as archetype—while varying possibilities within its organisation. This is not so much an individualisation for each owner as an articulation for each condition seen generically: the classical rhetorical trope is to classify 'variety in unity', and this figure has conditioned the design.

CJ

This building on the corner of a small residential block in Berlin constitutes an attempt to create an architecture that grows out of the existing situation, out of the specific nature of the site, the chance composition of the existing structure. This is an architecture for a very determinate place, in which what is already there and what is added, the old and the new, are interchangeable, blending with and commenting on each other. The existing old building, a U-shaped block of houses, is completed by a construction of approximately the same size, also in the shape of a U. The two blocks together enclose a newly created court.

The theme of the architecture has been defined in its spatial complexity and in the organisation of its layout on the basis of the existing fragment. In this fragment is contained the principle of a surrounding wall in which the dwellings are set. This principle has been taken up in the new construction as the dominant theme. In the surrounding wall itself the potential themes of the wall have been varied. The range of these variations stretches from the ideal form through its gradual transformation into openings in the wall and finally into individual buildings that are set independently in front of the wall.

The play of variations of the architectural form is resumed in the design of the facade. The neutral term of entrance for example, is precisely stated as door, entrance, portal; the general term of window is interpreted as a row of windows, a bay-window, a niche or a front of windows; the facade is divided up into base, middle part, and architrave. The principle of large-scale repetition of the facade of the old building is contrasted by the shifted scale in the newly constructed part, almost creating an effect of optical illusion.

Analogous to the plan, also in the building's facade, chance and calculation, the existing and the planned, are interchangeable. It is an attempt, by the use of the principle of interchange-ability, of ambivalence, to enhance the reality in a creative sense, thus relativising the spatial and stylistic inter-dependencies.

At the same time the principle of assimilation or of adaption to the existing situation, and the reflections that result from it, lead to a differentiation of the architectural design. By differentiation, is meant the introduction of poetics into the architectural language, which is thereby freed from the constraints of generalisation and from the reduction to the lowest common denominator of reality. This makes possible a dialogue between the different components—the new ones and the old, what exists and what may potentially be. Such a dialogue can only take place when what is already there and what is planned work together and complete each other.

In this conception of architecture, the old and the new are of equal value. They should not be seen as antagonistic elements, but as elements that are mutually interdependent, conditioning each other like exhalation and inhalation. So the theme of assimilation leads to the reaffirmation of a living architecture in contrast to a way of building which is petrified in dogma.

Oswald Mathias Ungers

12 Interior of courtyard showing elevated gardens. A dense staccato beat of windows, signifying different interior transformations, is set against a minimal wall surface which makes the intensity of surface more pronounced. The relation of solid to void, and the abstraction of rhythmical orders—bay rhythms—seems to be a consequence of interior decisions. (ph Waltraud Kräse)

O M UNGERS

Frankfurt Fair Hall and Galleria, Frankfurt-am-Main, 1979–82

1 Perspective from the main street shows the tiers of staccato elements and a flat roof for parking. The wide-open blue sky is now a regular feature of Ungers' *vedute*. Like eighteenth-century topographical painters, Canaletto and Bellotto, he uses a white-blue sky above a wide-angled view to suggest a world open to pleasure and exploration.

2 View of arrival point by car or bus, the galleria to the left and row of entrances extending down the long 'front'. (ph Waltraud Kräse)

3 Extreme repetition, like that of Late-Modernists and Aldo Rossi, results in an 'architecture of shadows' for the many entrances. Planters await their cypresses. (ph Waltraud Kräse)

2

3

Geometrical Platonism

Four architectural 'themes' are resolved here by the abstract grid: 1 the galleria; 2 shed or warehouse; 3 stepped platform; 4 parking field. The four-foot square, a unit of measure and order, dominates throughout. As in other schemes, Ungers orders the sub-themes, but lets the overall order of the facade rhythms be determined by internal function. Thus each horizontal level, coloured with the ruddy brown pigment common to Frankfurt buildings, is an independent theme in itself.

The most extraordinary opposition in Ungers' typical coincidentum oppositorum *is that between the 'heavenly vault' and the 'materialistic shed', the dialectic between Plato and Aristotle. The vault is a type based on the Galleria Umberto I in Naples and London's Crystal Palace (1851), which also had crossbraces. Here, however, the Platonic roof is a 'tension arch', itself*

4

a contradiction, or at least opposition between usual structural forces. As can be seen, vertical loads that come down to the springing of the wooden arch are then taken laterally by diagonal, steel members to one of the four main pylons. These are gigantic, Adamesque fan lights. A very airy rhythm is set up between each pylon as the number of diagonal braces increases towards the support.

The shed, or warehouse, space is something of a monster, as are all the Frankfurt leviathans. As a building type it reflects that overconcentration which has plagued fairs since the nineteenth century. The Frankfurt Book Fair is notoriously un-fair-like, or unfunny, but nonetheless mandatory for publishers. In Ungers' building, as in the others, financial pragmatism has forced a mixture of megasize, if that is a suitably ugly word, and sandwich space. Here the boredom is mediated by the

5

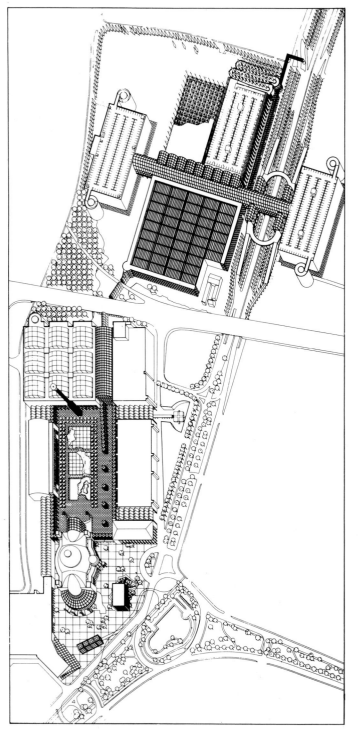

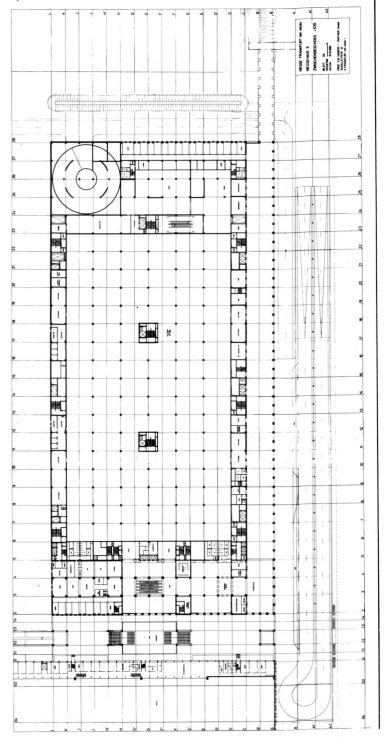

variety of internal spaces and the galleria link. Also the red concrete block acts as a traditional sign of decoration, even rustication, and, if the money is forthcoming, cypress trees will occupy the planters.

Now the image of the shed is that of a fortress with crenellations and also that of a Neo-Classical, perspective street, relating to those of Weinbrenner and Leo von Klenze. Like Aldo Rossi, Ungers repeats a pylon incessantly and hypnotically. As with Boullée the taste is for a megalomaniacal 'architecture of shadows' where the dark and light alternations have replaced ornament. In this building type, perhaps the sublime monotony is most appropriate, and it was, of course, a virtue in the nineteenth century.

Finally, however, it is the contrasts which provoke a response of admiration: glass set against masonry, swelling vertical curve versus gunshot horizontal, straight, open-plan centre versus closed-plan perimeter, open-sky platform—the Aztec altar—versus tight office space. In uniting the Modernist expression of structure with the traditional idealist expression of geometrical type, Ungers is resolving these contrasts at a large, if not small, scale.

CJ

4 Axonometric of the competition entry; the Ungers' addition is on the left with the galleria linking two parking structures and another 'shed' to the south.
5 Plan showing the variety of 'type' spaces: galleria, arrival point, open space, enclosed offices, arcade space, etc.
6 Perspective of galleria.
7 Site plan.

6

7

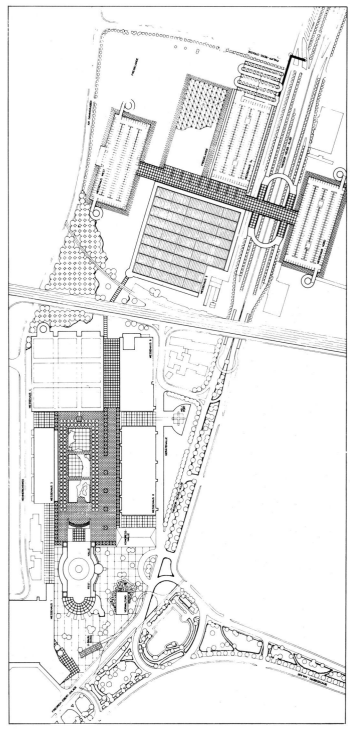

8 Laminated wood trusses with steel tension members pulling towards the Adamesque supports. (ph Waltraud Kräse)

9 Side of hall, showing random order, or the combination of sub-theme order with no *a priori* compositional order. (ph Jencks)

10 Ludwigstrasse, Munich (1815–40) by Leo von Klenze with buildings in the foreground by Friedrich Gartner. Since 1800, extreme repetition and foreshortening have been a consequence of the 'go street', a place where the aesthetics of pragmatism and the sublime converge. (ph Jencks)

TOYOKAZU WATANABE

Nakano House, 1979, Okamuro House, 1981 and Sugiyama House, 1980

Logical Classicism

These three modest houses show control and a strong sensibility. Paradoxical, suspended between Modernism, classicism and Buddhism—as Watanabe mentions in his summary of Adolf Loos—they are clear propositions of architecture. Perhaps they remain too primitive and raw, not to mention reverberant in concrete, but powerful they are. Reminiscent of Loos' apartment houses, and his aphorism that architecture resides in the tomb and monument, they also resemble the stupa, the mandala. Thus an extreme form of abstract symbolism and logic unites opposite cultures. The archetypal form is common to Western classicism and subsequent architectures.

CJ

2

Paradox and reverse in the works of Adolf Loos (summary)

No architect in the pre-Modern period adhered like Adolf Loos to cubical forms and planar surfaces. But his architecture had a strongly classical feeling, which was not necessarily of ancient Greece or Rome, but related more to the gravity of Egyptian sanctuaries. And certain buildings of Loos have a kind of schizoid feeling which comes from the juxtaposition of the classical or traditional elements with modern ones. This might be thought a transitional phenomenon of a European moving into the Modern period. But this interpretation doesn't sufficiently explain the subtle charms of his work. So, I investigated some of his buildings and projects, hoping to discover the origin of this complex charm: the Kärntner Bar, the project for the Chicago Tribune, Grabmal Max Dvořák, the House in the Michaelerplatz, and the Steiner House.

1

3
4

The study focuses on the mirrors in the Kärntner Bar and on the metaphor of the mirror expounded in the Kegon sect of Buddhism. It then analyses the conflict between the classical and modern by relating it analogically with the relation between the virtual image in a mirror and the real world. In effect, the subject of my essay relates the secrets of Loos' buildings to the cosmology of the mirror as expounded by the Kegon sect.

1 Adolf Loos, Projekt für ein Wohnhaus der Gemeinde, Vienna, 1920, stepped row-housing in terraces with a slight curve and classical rhythms.
2 Toyokazu Watanabe, *Nakano House*, Hyogo, 1978. Symmetry and setbacks of the tomb. Monumental construction. (ph Hitoshi Kawamoto)
3 Toyokazu Watanabe, *Okamuro House*, Yamatokoriyama, Nara, 1981. (ph Hitoshi Kawamoto)
4 Toyokazu Watanabe, *Sugiyama House*, Higashiosaka, Osaka, 1980. (ph Hitoshi Kawamoto)

Nakano House (Standard House 001)
Takarazuka, Hyogo, Japan, 1979

Reminiscent of other Japanese work, particularly Aida's Nirvana House of 1972, this extremely simple statement achieves its power through slight shifts in proportions. It might be a five-storey building with setbacks rising gradually to a central crescendo. But in fact, it is a series of boxes telescoped within each other in a continuous space—essentially a one-storey building with an interior pagoda. Typically, Watanabe stresses the central route, the mysterious procession up a dark stairway to the culmination in an abstract sky. Tomb, pagoda, chapel to abstraction—the painter's house is a shrine to metaphysical speculation.

CJ

This is a painter's house and although it has only a minimum number of rooms (one bedroom, kitchen, bathroom and wc), the client can freely partition it. The form of this house came from the image of a tomb, since the origins of the house may be in the tomb. This tomb-like house expresses itself as the most primitive archetype. The name 'Standard House 001' refers to the fact that modern architecture might have minimum spatial standards before partitions are added.

Toyokazu Watanabe

1 Plans and elevations.
2 View from the street.
3 The central sunwell.
4 The way up is usually from dark to light.
5 The painter's space: square windows push up against the ceilings as in the top of a pagoda.
All photos Hitoshi Kawamoto.

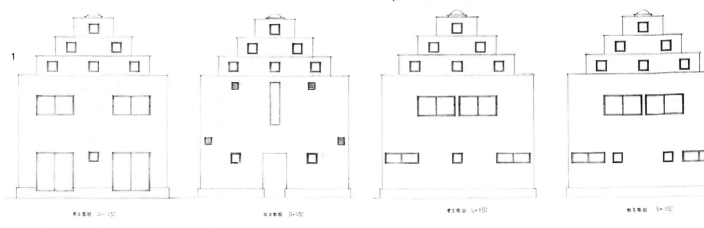

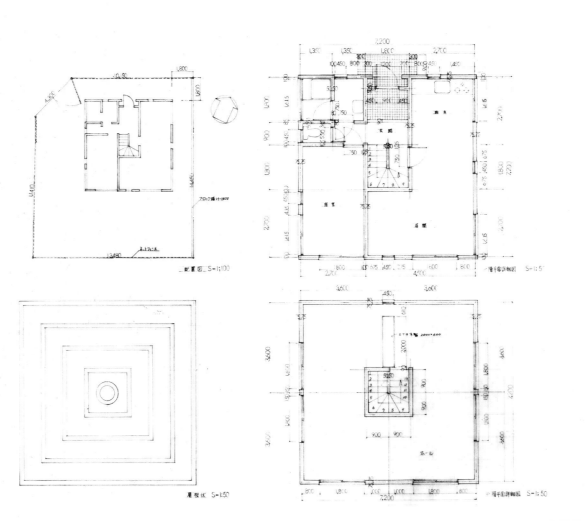

2
4

3
5

Okamuro House
Yamatokoriyama, Nara, Japan, 1981

The Okamuro House is a mysterious, not to say, hallucinatory combination of a dome (dropped from the sky) and a suburban house. These two images literally interpenetrate in a way that recalls the overlapping spaces of Baroque and Modernism alike. This typical Post-Modern hybrid has been given an extreme hieratic ordering. There is the split oval, a trompe l'oeil reminiscent at once of Brunelleschi's use of pietra serena and Nervi's isostatic lines of force. Geometry and restrained decoration have unified dualities and made the unlikely combinations appear quite natural.   CJ

This house, for an ordinary, salaried man, is on a site surrounded by the traditional landscape of the old capital of Nara.

Hence the quiet appearance of the exterior, which honours the landscape, and, to compensate, the interior which is quite unique. The dome, confined within the house, is the most emphatic expression. The curved glass in the fissure of the dome opens to the sky, and rain comes down there. It is nice to see foggy rain through the glass.

Toyokazu Watanabe

1 Sections.
2 Plans.
3 Split oval dome.
4 View up gable of real and virtual stairway.
5 Three fundamentalist columns acting as screen.
6 (overleaf) Real and virtual lines of force in black.
All photos by Hitoshi Kawamoto.

1

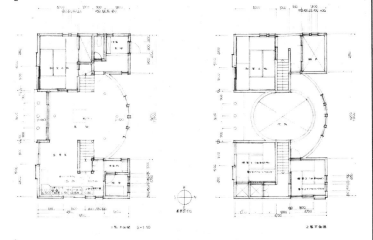

2

3

4

Sugiyama House
Higashiosaka, Osaka, Japan, 1980

This house appears much larger than it really is because of the strange distortions of customary cues, especially the suggestion of a storied ziggurat, or perhaps a row house by Adolf Loos. The dark, square window is used at different scales and in odd places (sometimes on the floor), also to augment the size. Amplification combined with the rhetorical trope of extreme simplicity make the familiar become unfamiliar and therefore artistic.

The building is as terse as Watanabe's statements, laconic like the dialogues of Beckett or Pinter; we may read inflections into near silences. Harsh and noble, brutal and elevated in its aloof posture (what is it like to inhabit the attic-studio of this ziggurat?) the house is more coolly ambiguous than Watanabe's previous ironic Post-Modernism (which combined Le Corbusier and Michelangelo). Contradictions are absorbed within archetypal presences—the repeated gable-shape, the repeated square window, the repeated rectangular floor. As with so many architects today, Watanabe is returning to a pre-Modern synthesis, that of stripped, constructional classicism.

CJ

This is the house of another painter who consistently paints abstract pictures only in black. For him, living in the darkness, a house might be in the state of an unfinished perpetuality: hence the image of a built ruin, or the story of a man who dwells in a ruined castle. On the third floor is an atelier, on the second the rooms for the client and his wife and children, and on the first is the room of his old mother.

Toyokazu Watanabe

1 Street side.
2–5 Plan, section and elevations.
6 Field side with asymmetrical symmetry.
7 Entrance with cruciform sign and repeated triangular gable.
8 Reversible floor and ceiling; turn the page upside-down and the image works because of the few visual cues.
9 Stair and column are virtual, not real.
10 Painter's studio with primary forms. Not visible are the windows in the floor.
All photos by Hitoshi Kawamoto.

1

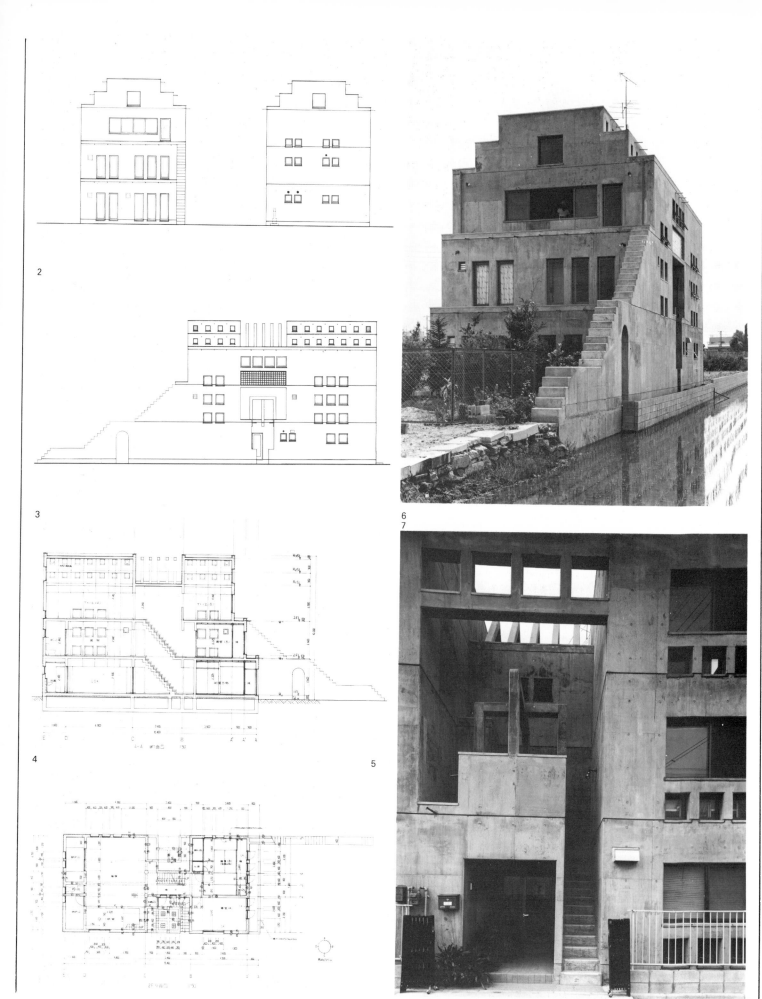

2

3

4

5

6
7

54

8

9

10

TERADA, TAKEYAMA & UNITED ACTIONS

Building No 10, Musashino Art University, 1982

Ironic Opposition

A certain irony can be detected in Takeyama's conjunction of attitudes, 'Koten and Klassik', which he describes below. His building also shows a severe opposition of Modernist construction and classicist archetypes. The resultant mixture is abstract, in spite of its imagery, and fundamentalist, in spite of Takeyama's praise of Murano's metaphors. Perhaps this restraint is a result of the budget and restrictions imposed by the client. In any case, it underlines, once again, the fact that certain similarities do exist between classicism and Modernism on the level of construction and order, while their significance is opposite in terms of ideals and reference. This clarifies the opposition between Murano's and Tange's 'Klassik'—one inclusive to the point of kitsch, the other exclusive to the point of prohibition. Since it is Takeyama's intention to unite opposites in a dialectical manner, one might have expected the dualism of his statement, ultimately an irony unified by the overpowering geometry of the building.

CJ

Minoru Takeyama
Koten and/or Klassik

Koten and/or Klassik—the basic pattern of recent Japanese classicism

The terminology of classicism is doubly coded in Japanese: *Koten* and *Klassik*. When the Japanese use the word *Koten* (*Ko* = old; *Ten* = writing or rules), it refers mostly to Japanese traditional classicism, while the word *Klassik* refers to Western, or non-Japanese classicism.

Koten does not always symbolise the traditional master work, but it does imply a process of creation which an eminent predecessor has maintained to achieve a great work. The *Koten* product is a sign which denotes an admirable process of creation. *'To look after what the master looked for'* is a discipline which has been customarily preserved in traditional Japanese creativity in any genre. Here *'what the master looked for'* is not the predecessor's solutions, but the process of his patient search, or the manner of his pursuit.

Koten, therefore, does not entail the use of any particular style, or essence, but keeps the successor's attitude on the right tracks through the preconceived discipline. *Klassik*, on the other hand, has been used as a label to distinguish the Western classical styles from the Japanese. *Klassik* is simply a synonym for Western classicism. For example, *Klassik* music refers to Bach and Beethoven whereas *Koten* music is limited to the Japanese such as Koto (a kind of harp) or Shakuhachi (flute); this music did not have the usual notation and was performed *ad lib* among the *Koten* players. The same goes for architecture. *Koten* always remains within the text book of the history of Japanese architecture, while *Klassik* is in that of Western architecture. Both architectural histories were described respectively in different text books until recently, when the direct transplantation of Western classicism took place in monumental public buildings.

Today, the ruling taste of the public in our homogenous society has accepted a very heterogenous living environment. The boundary between Japanese and non-Japanese has been virtually eliminated. Fifty years ago, a Japanese visitor would have been surprised to watch American kids playing baseball while their mouths were busy chewing gum. Today, some Japanese children who believe that both baseball and chewing gum are of Japanese origin would be surprised to find American boys playing the Japanese national sport and enjoying the Japanese product in their mouths.

Dissimilarity between the East and West in terms of visual expression is more rare than similarity for today's mass-culture. As the mass-culture has been enriched and 'the empire of signs' consequently become kaleidoscopic, the boundary between *Koten* and *Klassik* has been lost. Now, it has become possible to realise *Koten* even with *Klassik* styles and forms. Japanese classicism is extremely hybrid; in most cases the content is authentically Japanese and the expression is Western. It is the Kimono mind in Western costume. One of the most remarkable examples of *Koten* and/or *Klassik* seems to be the Prince Hotel which the master-builder Togo Murano (born 1891) recently completed in Tokyo.

1   2

1 Togo Murano, The Prince Hotel, Tokyo, 1982. The Convention Hall, named by a poet as *Hiten* (flying in the sky), has many more meanings than this metaphorical one. The architect's intention was to convey the tranquillity of the deep sea: something he has achieved in part by pasting 300,000 pieces of mother-of-pearl on the ceiling, and by the marine-like lights. The curved form is also multivalent, relating to Gothic, Persian and Buddhist forms (praying hands). (ph Takeyama)
2 Kenzo Tange, The Prince Hotel, Tokyo, 1983. Symmetrical, but within the univalent codes of Modernism. (ph Takeyama)

Coincidentally, Kenzo Tange, born in 1913 and graduated from Tokyo university in 1938, is also doing another Prince Hotel in Tokyo, expected to be completed in 1983. The comparison between the two might support my viewpoint on Japanese classicism. Tange's hotel is exclusive, by intentionally making no effort to cope with heterogeneous languages. The solution is very univalent, and Tange justifies this architectural syntax in an urban context which is already multivalent. There is no single sign of classicism, but a strong linkage to the tradition of Modernism.

By contrast, Murano's hotel is extremely inclusive. His polyphonic orchestration, performed at the age of 91, goes beyond the boundary between *Koten* and *Klassik*, Modern and Classic, East and West, all the contradictory demands caused by the opposite codes of architectural language.

After I visited the sites of both buildings with my students, one of them remarked: '*Tange's hotel is for VIP businessmen only, the Murano only for honeymooners*'. Another student exclaimed: '*I feel so close to the Tange, because I think I could do the same. But the Murano is fantastic; the taste and solutions, all far beyond my reach!*'

* * *

A work of my own, Studio Building No 10, illustrates the two aspects of classicism. It is an extension to the existing campus of the Musashino Art Institute in Tokyo. The campus planning was done by Ashihara (architect and the author of *Exterior Space*) and most of the buildings have already been built.

The site was at the north-east corner of the campus and in the near future through traffic is expected to run right next to it. After completion, it will attract most of the outsiders' attention. Considering this future plan, my initial proposal was to make a symbolic building by combining the school symbol, an ideograph of fine art, with the requested space organisation. The circular site was sunken and the linear skylight was shaped in the character of 'Beauty', the school symbol, so that people could read the mark from the outside, especially at night. This ideographic proposal was however luckily cancelled by Ashihara because of its lack of continuity with the rest of the campus. The humour of my intention was not absolutely accepted. The clients asked me to follow strictly the syntax of the neighbouring Building No 9; the width and the height, the size of windows, the edge of building, the finish of exposed concrete, the structural framework of 4.8 x 9.6m modules, and the circulation pattern of the double corridors. In sum, the client demanded an almost identical building. How to win this losing game? I took advantage of the client's restrictions. *Koten* and/ or *Klassik* has proved to be the effective solution: 'small exterior, large interior', or 'poor outside, rich inside', a manner of *Koten* space composition together with some *Klassik* flavour around. The pillars with square bases, the triangular end-wall, altar-like terrace, and flower-shaped benches are all *Klassik* fragments, although they are bleached and covered with white tiles so that the art students can easily organise their colourful exhibitions in this white space.

The space between the double corridors was entirely eliminated to make a sort of atrium. The concrete truss was put on without having a glass roof, but various devices exist from which students can hang any objects for exhibition. In the middle an elm tree was proposed but it has remained unplanted because the clients thought it might remind visitors of a commercial shopping mall.

Compared with the unbuilt proposal, this solution has become more independent from the rest of the campus due to the *Koten* and/or *Klassik* manner, a newer dimension of the hybrid codes of architecture.   *Minoru Takeyama*

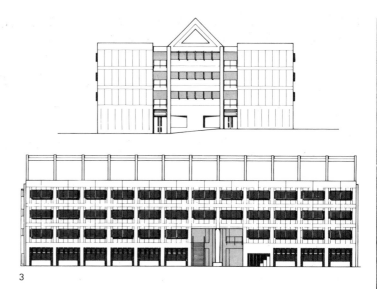

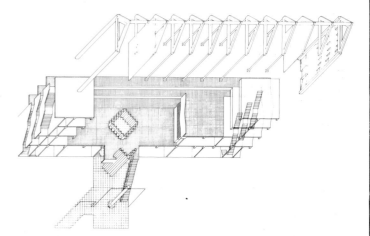

3

4

5

3 Elevations.
4 Exploded axonometric of the 'atrium' and repeated triangular motif.
5 Axonometric.

6 Interior of the atrium. (ph Katsuaki Furudate)

7 Studio Building No 10, Musashino Art Institute, east elevation. (ph Katsuaki Furudate)

NEW
REPRESENTATION

Studio Nizzoli (Oliveri, Susini, Viola), *New Editorial Domus offices*, near Milan, 1980–82. The front, like Tigerman's housing, pages 78–79, represents an Ionic column and window-wall. The back, quite opposite, is a cascade in brick. Taken as a partial and distorted sign—of sunken column, face and plant holder—it has an enigmatic but potent presence.

VENTURI, RAUCH & SCOTT BROWN

Private House, Greenville, Delaware, 1978–82

Silhouette Classicism

Overscaled pediments, lunettes and Doric columns are cut out and used as appliqué. Even the interior 'Gothic' vault is rendered as an insubstantial silhouette. This amplification in size and diminishment in section creates a very tense impression, as if the classical language (and the building) were being stretched to their limits. The notion of cut-out paper dolls is not far away. And what was once a beautiful set of proportions in stone—permanent, solid, substantial—is here made transitory, paper-thin and fragmented. It may be an ugly jumble when looked at through Neo-Classical, or Rationalist spectacles, since rhythms and shapes collide, but it has a harmony, even prettiness, when seen as a Queen Anne Revival, or Free Style Classical, composition.

The large-scale pediments, set below the eaves on both faces, unify the heterogeneous shapes and indicate the large, honorific music room. The white trim and stencilled ornament are as pretty as any Queen Anne daintiness. The sectioned Doric is a rather beautiful residue of the wall, actually walking off the wall, by degrees. In an early Doric Temple at Paestum the fat column was placed 'incorrectly' on the main axis—and so it is here, with a knowingness borne out by the other witty solecisms.

Note the clever interlocking of space, with extra rooms squeezed under the attic, while the ceremonial music room with its central axis is allowed to impress itself on the outside. The drawings indicate a commitment to a geometric order which is always present, no matter how many times interrupted. Indeed, the whole building represents classicism interrupted, or rambled, or jumbled, as if Stanford White were playing International Style jazz with white horizontals and vernacular shingle. CJ

This is a house for a family of three. The wife is a musician—a performer who needs a music room containing an organ, two pianos, and a harpsichord. This room should also be appropriate for small gatherings. Another interest of the family is birdwatching so that big windows facing the woods, especially in the breakfast area, are important. The husband needs a study in a remote part of the house, and the nine-year-old son his own apartment.

The house sits in rolling fields at the edge of a valley towards the west with woods towards the north. Traditional to eastern Delaware, where the site is located, are eighteenth-century classical barns with generous scale and low horizontal proportions—almost Palladian in character. They contain low porches set into the bulk of the building with stout columns, pent-eaves, and squat openings, all of which increase the horizontal emphasis of the building. The walls of these barns are field stone with areas of wood frame and siding in the upper sections. We based the form of the house and its symbolism on this kind of indigenous architecture to make it look at home within its rural setting and to conform to the easy, generous, yet unpretentious way of living that our clients envisioned.

We substituted stucco on block for masonry on the outside and our columns are flat and stylised representations of the Doric Order. Over the front pediment is an ornamental screen reminiscent of a Baroque lunette in Salzburg; it is where the big music room is and it acts to enhance the scale of this side of the house when seen from a distance as you approach over the field. On the other side is a more classical lunette screen over columns 1½ storeys high which increase the scale of the house from across the valley.

Although you do not enter from the centre, the plan is organised around a central axis; on each side of this axis in plan and elevation the symmetry breaks down to accommodate particular requirements of the programme. The library and the hall which contains the dining table are on axis on the ground floor. Although the music room dominates the plan in the same way on the second floor, it is remote because it is usually closed off to maintain temperature and humidity control for the sake of the musical instruments there; its big windows are set back to diminish the sun-load. In section, the music room is a high space with a latticed groin vault with Carpenter-Gothic proportions. This room dominates the front and rear elevations of the house too by its central location, but its big pediments, front and back, do not intrude on the silhouette of the whole of the house. You normally enter this country house through the kitchen door where there is an overhang under which to unload the back of a station wagon. The garage is a separate outbuilding with storage above. The landscaping is cultivated in the immediate vicinity of the house, but natural beyond. Inside the ornament consists of flat, silhouetted representations in wood of the classical ornament of the eighteenth and nineteenth centuries in this part of the world.

Venturi, Rauch and Scott Brown

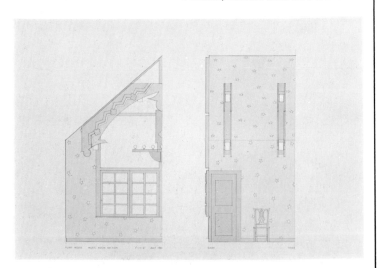

1
1 Music room section showing 'Gothic' arch with its pink quatrefoils and broken chevrons in pale green, yellow, red and grey. Note also the white stars—Venturi has written about ornament breaking up the structure and tectonic expression, as in a Romanesque dome.
2 View from the east with the large roof coming down close to the ground, as in Lutyens' Homewood, to make the scale more domestic.
3 South view showing garage, left, and large-scale pediments above the trellised entrance. The simple plan is expressed in the roof.

2
3

61

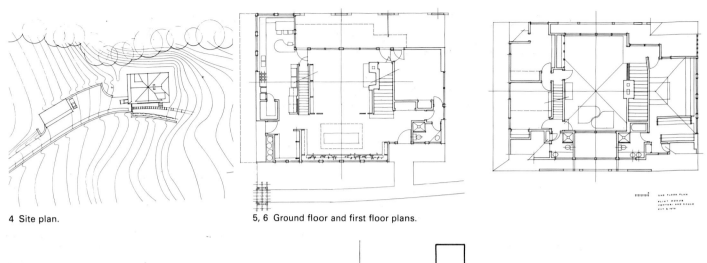

4 Site plan.

5, 6 Ground floor and first floor plans.

7 Section looking west showing superimposition of scales.

8 West elevation with its Paestum Doric as a sectioned elevation walking off the wall.

VENTURI, RAUCH & SCOTT BROWN

Studio, Block Island, New York, 1980–82

Circumstantial Classicism

These two modest structures carry on the Venturian tradition of mixing opposites: the informal and formal, the big and small and above all the circumstantial and classical. Contingent functional requirements such as the placement of windows and 'front' door have led to an informal, picturesque order, while the overall compositional principles—symmetry, pitched roof on rectangular axis, simple geometry—are classical. Explicit classical references such as the fanlight and pedimental triangles underline the variations all the more: the inconsistent use of mullions, the dramatic shift in window size, the asymmetries. Thus the strongest Free Style Classical rules are present—asymmetrical symmetry, the 'double/single', the monumental vernacular—all oxymoronic figures. Most paradoxical of all, to those acquainted with eighteenth-century Cape Cod houses, are the steeply pitched roof and high vertical column, for these characterise this old type and make the 'double/single' into the 'old-fashioned/new'. That this is intentional can be seen in the wicker furniture and wood burning stove, both of which are presented in a way which is almost straight. Only the odd windows and jarringly proportioned bookshelves indicate the new. And yet even these elements were often placed in naive relationship with each other—smashing up into the ceiling, hitting each other without transition—in the eighteenth century.

So we have a comment on this type, the 'charmingly odd', which declares itself more an heir to a tradition which is native, than to Modernism. It's an exemplary Shock of the Old.

CJ

The programme for these two big/little buildings on Block Island is very simple. The larger building has living, dining and kitchen on the ground floor and a studio above in the gable; the smaller building has a garage workshop below, with two guest rooms above. The site is an open meadow running down to a salt-water pond.

The stylistic source for these buildings is the countrified Classic Revival which was typical of many nineteenth-century buildings on Block Island. Unlike the New England salt box tradition with its small-size windows, asymmetrical gables, and small-scale details, the Classic Revival bungalow had a 'Temple Front' with symmetrical entrance; a simple profile with over-scaled overhangs, windows, batterboards and trim. These big/little buildings use an ordinary historical image and associations combined with big-scale elements to create an extraordinary monumental presence which belies their small size.

Venturi, Rauch and Scott Brown

1 View from the south-west showing the front symmetries modified by the inset door. The giant fanlight and variously scaled window panes give movement to a very formal composition.

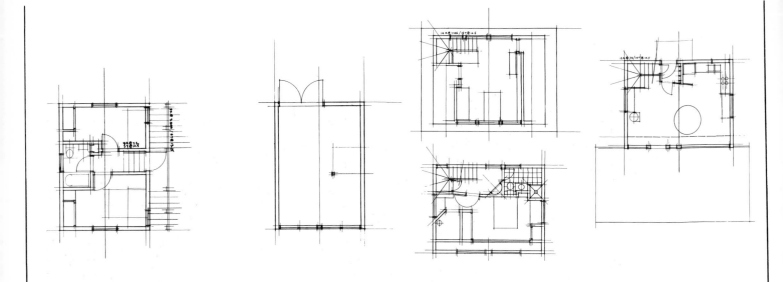

2

4

3

5
6

2, 3 Plans and elevations of the small house. Note in all these drawings the emphasis on centering lines, the classical ordering by axes and rhythms.

4, 5, 6 Plans, sections and elevations of the large house. The absolute axis is emphasised, then denied.

7
8

7 View from the north-west of the 'back door'. Here the asymmetries predominate. The mixture of white trim and shingle is conventional on Block Island.
8 Corner storage emphasises, in an understated way, classical voids and primary geometry; pale yellows and oranges are set against white to underscore these points.
9 Living/dining room and its large windows open over the view; note the orange floorboards, the ladder-back rocking chair and wood-burning stove set against the asymmetrical grid.

All photos Venturi, Rauch and Scott Brown.
9

ROBERT STERN

Residence and Pool House, Llewelyn Park, New Jersey, 1981–82

Gargantuan Classicism

Heavy, muscle-bound Tuscan columns hold rusticated streamlines that anchor the Neo-Colonial building to its site. This marrying of the building to the earth with Wrightian streamlines is done so emphatically, with such masculine finality, that one is relieved to find, on the inside of the poolhouse, the dancing-women keystones and very light Secessionist ornament. This sets the mood for splashing and diving. Indeed the interior, with its syncopation of blues and whites, with its shimmering colours and reflective surfaces, its sparkling light from many sources, is a convincing metaphor of bodily regeneration. If that is the subject towards which the Art Deco plan swivels, then it is a climax made fitting with rhetorical motifs. One turns and cascades down flowing steps, past a figure leaning forward pouring water—the 'water-boy'—and then through a split column down more Art Deco staggers (repeated across the roof) to a double curved stair à la Philibert de l'Orme to the final plunge into a mysterious ultramarine blue. Nash and Hollein have supplied the metal palm trees; Hejduk, Tigerman and Farrell have helped with the animal-cracker roof profile; Lutyens worked on a similar shrunken/overblown classicism—yet it's all unmistakably in the Stern eclectic manner. A diagrammatic, abstract aspect relates it to his Modernist training, as do the fashionable 15° shifts on the second-floor library wall. Very strange indeed are the bloated, blob poché elements: is this the beginning of a new Expressionist Classicism? It's as if poché were now turned inside out and used positively as a figure in space rather than, as usual, as a background-forming space.

CJ

Residence for Mr and Mrs Albert Cohn, Llewellyn Park, New Jersey, under construction

This project consists of two components: the renovation of a Georgian house designed in 1929 by Edgar Williams, and the addition of alterations to the terraces and garden to accommodate a new tennis court and a new structure housing an indoor swimming pool. The renovation of the original structure responds to the owners' needs for more living space and less servants' quarters and to a feeling that the character of the original interior space was pompous. In reordering the interiors a syncopated counterpoint emerges between what appears to be, though is not necessarily, old and new. This is particularly vivid on the first floor where a new classically composed columnar order is introduced to counterpoint the free curves of the screen wall that encloses the living room. It can also be seen on the second floor where a sweeping diagonal ties together space in the principal part of the house with that in what was formerly the servants' wing.

The pool house is deliberately complex in its formal references—a good-time place cloaked in an envelope that responds to the character of the original house while at the same time taking on the character of a landscape feature: it is a kind of grotto or nymphaeum that marks a transition between the house, its terraces, and the garden. The palm tree columns that carry the terrace recall John Nash's at the Brighton Pavilion.

These columns are used in a way similar to that used by Hans Hollein in a travel office in Vienna—to trigger appropriate and pleasant thoughts of sun-filled tropical islands. The tile walls induce a subaqueous character to the room. The use of faux-marble pilasters of almost archaic character are a complement to the various high-tech strategies employed to capture solar heat and natural light and to open the pool to the garden.

Robert Stern

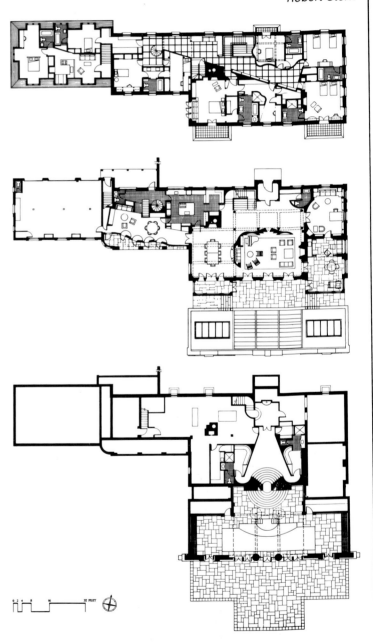

1 Ground floor plan. Note the double curved stair from Philibert de l'Orme and the forced perspective focusing on the 'water-boy'.
2 First floor plan shows reverse *poché* and, to left, the meandering glass wall.
3 Second floor plan with 15° shifted wall of books.

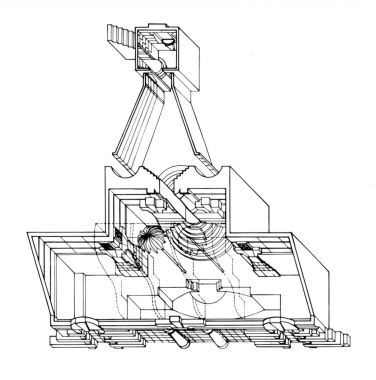

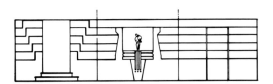

VESTIBULE

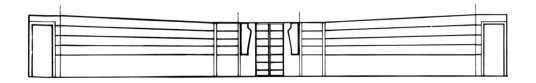

HALL

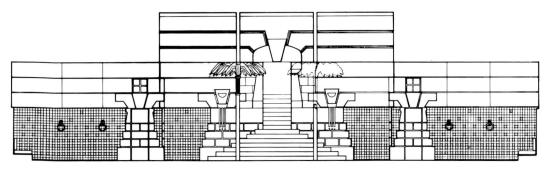

INTERIOR ELEVATION

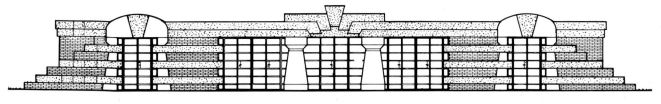

EXTERIOR ELEVATION

4 Poolhouse axonometric and elevations.

5

6

7

8

9

10

5 Poolhouse door with its gargantuan, cantilevered, streamlined rustication repeats the horizontality of the roof. (ph E Stoecklein)

6 Poolhouse rustication marries the Neo-Colonial house to the earth. (ph E Stoecklein)

7 Rusticated bookcase with shifted axis and Modernist abstraction. (ph E Stoecklein)

8 Lutyensesque ovoid and Art Deco stagger which spins one towards the 'water-boy' and the final plunge. (ph E Stoecklein)

9 The staggers of the roof pull the space down to give a low scale; dancing women with keystones lighten the corners. (ph Norman McGrath)

10 The temple to bodily regeneration is, finally, rather Egyptian in feeling. (ph Norman McGrath)

VOORSANGER & MILLS

Le Cygne Restaurant, New York City, 1981–82

This haute cuisine *restaurant creates a fresh feeling of opening out into space in spite of being almost totally enclosed. This is partly due to the expansive, vertical vestibule, the use of multiple light sources, planting,* trompe l'oeil *windows at different scales, and the subtle gradation of naturalistic colours such as the sky blue. In short, architectural illusion is used to counteract a potentially oppressive architectural fact. All this light-filled complexity is controlled by the repetition of an abstract grid and hieratic ordering: the procession around a central space and the strong emphasis on symmetry. Subtle changes in colour accentuate both the layered space and figural shapes. Basic classical elements are stripped to essentials—no capitals, few mouldings—and the articulation of the facade in depth provides a pleasing classical anthropomorphic figure. Or perhaps it's more the presence of an animal we can feel in these protrusions and shadows. Thus as in Michael Graves' work, to which this scheme relates, the figural and representational elements are present but veiled.*

CJ

Le Cygne is a *haute cuisine* restaurant which has been relocated from its previous site next door, on Madison Avenue and 54th Street... The solution which emerged ... resulted in an extraordinary opportunity for us: a five-storey brownstone with all interior floors removed and programmatic requirements to replace only two of five floors within the interior volume...

Our intentions were to let the restaurant become a theatre of arrival, progression and destination. We deliberately decided therefore to keep both dining rooms [the main floor restaurant and second floor banquet room] modest in scale and to focus instead on the lobby as the driving force to attract customers to the second floor. We intended the second level to become a surrogate *piano nobile*, without diminishing the importance of the main floor.

The sequence of arrival and destination has been inverted. The four-storey lobby which normally would be 'arrival', becomes simultaneously the point of arrival and destination. It is only when the vertical section of the space becomes apparent that one realises the progression is renewed upward to a new destination: the second floor banquet rooms. (The second level eventually became an area so in demand that it is now being used exclusively for dining.)

To ensure that these rooms did not become fragments of space but remained connected, colour and detail became paramount. In this case, the mediating concept is Impressionism, an era in French history of extraordinary importance. During this period, the artist escaped the studio, moved to the outdoors, and was able to detail vividly throughout the day the effects of light upon objects and surfaces.

Accordingly, the lobby became—in terms of both light and strength of colour—the representation of 'mid-day'. The main dining room became 'morning', with its pale lavenders, blues and pinks. Upstairs became 'evening', with its lush warmth in pale pinks, oranges and ochres.

Voorsanger and Mills

1 Facade drawing (by R Velsor). This elevation of the five-storey brownstone recalls, as the architects describe it, the monumental scaling devices of Lars Sonck—a monumentality meant to relate to a 35-storey tower next door. The layering is chronological, beginning with a modulated granite base and returning to the brownstone and cornice of the original facade.

2

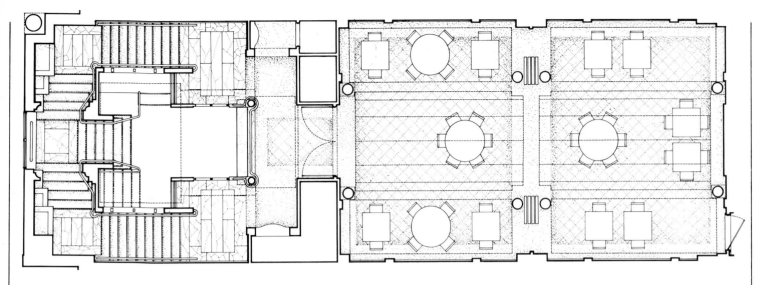

2 First floor plan.   3 Granite base with its symmetrical, anthropomorphic figure, square 'window' and protruding stair. (ph Jencks)   4 Ground floor plan.
5 (overleaf) View up vertical vestibule rising effectively four storeys. (ph © Peter Aaron, Esto Photographics Inc)

4

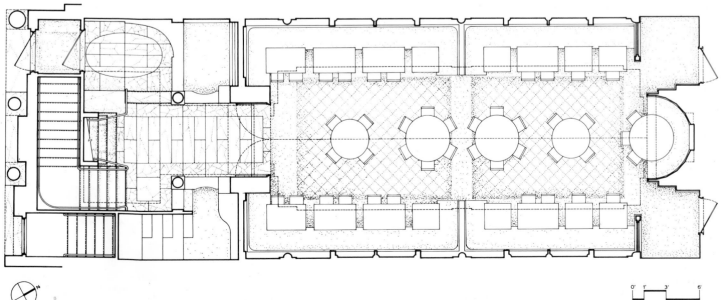

ACE

Figaro, Oakland, California, 1981–82

ACE Architects, with their representational name taken from the Ace of Spades, have pursued a form of representation that could be called 'compacted literalism'. Like Surrealists, they have taken everyday images and juxtaposed them within such a tight space and with such an ultra-realism that unlikely associations are forced onto the material. The House of Cards (built for Lucia Howard's family of bridge players) turns a dumb suburban house into an emblem of a current obsession in a way likely to set off a chain of opposite associations. The black club pediment—a voided lattice—surmounts the four suits, while the weathervane of revolving change rings the changes on another accident of fourness. One is reminded of Takefumi Aida's House like a Die—another fortuitous set of connections between a house and a game. In that building the game is played in a more thorough way than in the House of Cards—which dissipates the images with other suburban imagery.

The Hieroglyph Building, Ace's renovated office, attempts the eclectic definition of different spaces by giving each one a highly identifiable sign (or 'glyph'). The catholic opposition of images is most refreshing. The Wide Flange Table—a comment on Miesian skin and bones architecture—uses a powerful form of modern construction in a hieratic way and at a tiny scale. Furniture that resembles buildings, an old convention, is successful here because the transformation is well conceived and detailed. Less convincing, however admirable in intention, is the Egyptian Lobby, with its lotus capitals and 'jet black horii' (that look more like crucifixes). The problem is one of budget and detailing. When the desire for meaningful imagery outstrips both essentials, one is tempted to fall back on the Modernist position of neutral abstraction. This, ACE would say quite realistically, is the easiest and most evasive position in an age grown used to its agnosticism and lack of craftsmanship.

Their most accomplished, and most overwrought, building is the Figaro Ice Cream Parlour, a structure which features the Serliana (or Palladio's Vicenza Basilica motif). This exterior motif is repeated on the inside, and like the obelisks, multiplied by mirrors. To call this pretentious overstatement is to only half get the point: the commercial vernacular is precisely that. What else is going to attract the passerby, what else is blatant advertisement? Mixing this with sheet-metal Berninian columns and colours taken from John Soane's dining-room would normally upset purists, but they have no doubt become quite used to this sort of vulgarisation over the last ten years. Haute vulgarisation, if it can be done by Piranesi in his Egyptian-English tea room, is a possible approach to roadside architecture.

What is questionable is the identifiability of each image: literalism can undercut the appreciation of more profound meanings, the one-liner forecloses the second glance. Lucia Howard, in her text, has disputed this point and the force of her argument rests, I believe, on the hope that individual images may combine in a unique and displacing way. The more literal meanings are compacted together, the more surreal their interaction. Scale shifts, distortion by mirrors and the optical repetition of black

1 Figaro entrance to one side of Serliana and solomonic columns. (ph Rob Super)
2 Interior with *trompe l'oeil* and doubled image. (ph Rob Super)

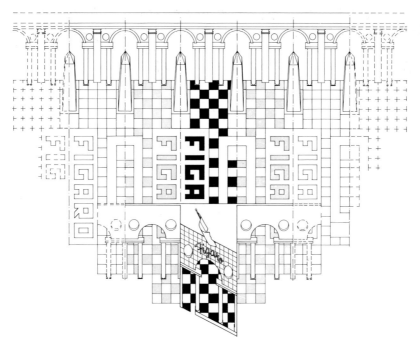

3 Conceptual up-elevation.

and white patterns—all these devices may help the displacement she seeks.

One might also add, as is the case in Pop Art, that such blatant imagery becomes paradoxically opaque, obscure, or at least beyond comment. The success of the building may thus finally rest on who is looking at it and in what mood. No doubt these architects have pushed representation in a more literal direction than Californians working in the same genre of explicit imagery—Eric Moss and Thomas Gordon Smith to name two opposites. It has become fashionable to dismiss this literalness as a typically Californian excess—at least Aldo Rossi and several Europeans tend to characterise the historicism this way. But at a time when traditional areas of expression have become taboo, or lost through inactivity, one can admire these architects for seeking to revive the conventional and public nature of symbolism. CJ

As a test case for our literal philosophy, Figaro has been illuminating. The original concept was rooted in representation. Yet the general public has added a large collection of readings beyond those intended. Though we were working with distinct images of Italian bars and the piazza at Vicenza, the rendition is both surreal and abstract enough to arouse recognition without completely prescribing what is to be recognised. People see their own experience mirrored in the architecture.

Figaro touches on numerous popular codes. We have been assured that Figaro is New Wave, Deco, Italian, high-tech, and even classical. Some see it as high toned and elegant, others as 'wonderfully sleazy'. We are pleased with this astonishing range of comparisons because it is not a 'one-liner', but evocative of many popular memories that cluster around bars and cafés or the pleasures of consuming special food and drink. The literalism of Figaro makes it accessible to a popular imagination.

I understand your point that our literalism may make our work seem one-dimensional. Reproduction is one-dimensional because it prescribes meaning. Yet our use of literalism is not like reproduction at all, but it is similar to representation. And representation, when rendered so that its readings are not restricted, elicits highly imaginative responses from ordinary people. Our use of representation is selective, and our rendition a trifle enigmatic. The objects represented are transformed, not reproduced. We have adopted this literalism as a polemic against things not understandable.

Lucia Howard

* * *

There is a particularly Italian talent for rendering the ordinary as the archetypal, for bringing out the sensually potent essences of everyday artifacts and experiences. With this, the commonplace is made vivid and potentially dramatic. This transformation involves techniques of simplification, exaggeration, and incantation, sometimes bravado hucksterism.

With Figaro, we have employed the first three of these (our critics accuse us of the last) to set the scene for those Italian alchemies surrounding the taking of espresso and gelati. These alchemies transform the former into the *idea* of coffee; they make of the latter the *pure sensation* of chocolate, strawberry, or vanilla. In both cases the archetypal is woven out of very ordinary fabric. These are mysteries (and techniques) like those celebrated (and employed) in the Roman Church, when common wafer and wine are made sacred body and blood. At Figaro, the setting, though not the setting's intention, is different.

Figaro is meant as a landscape of archetypes—obelisks, Palladian walls, the Italian flag, white chairs and tables: simplifications and exaggerations. All these, in collection, and with mirrors repeated infinitely, make for an idealised, dream-like piazza. As with a dream, this piazza is at once archetypal, because constituted of archetypes, and real, because inhabited. It is a piazza at once mysterious, because so little of it may be explored, and apparent, because so much of it is seen. In this piazza sounds, like images, are endlessly reflected. The hiss of steam from the espresso machine and the tenor's aria combine, transmuted and transformed in these reflections, becoming incantation.

Dreams make over reality, enhancing and suppressing the everyday, rendering it vivid. In the same way Figaro makes over a piazza, conjuring a landscape consonant with and encouraging the metamorphosis of espresso and gelati into idea and sensation. Drama is born of transformation, whether in the theatre, the Church, or an ice cream store. It is Figaro's special virtue to have worked this transformation on the commonplace, to have fashioned drama out of the ordinary.

Lucia Howard and David Weingarten

4
5

4 House of Cards, entrance, with four suits in columns and weathervane, diamond stair and club pediment.
5 Egyptian Lobby of Hieroglyph Building showing horii and lotus capitals. (ph Rob Super)
6 Wide Flange Table in Hieroglyph Building fabricated from steel 'I' sections, tubes and plates and topped with stainless steel edged wire glass—all sections dipped in molten zinc. (ph Rob Super)

6

ACE

El Rancho Rio, Carmel, California, 1979–80

The Shock of Recognition

For most of this century the formal part of architectural design has been thought a pretty abstract matter. Designers have conceived of buildings as abstract forms manipulated to create certain effects and to accommodate programme and circumstance. At Ace Design we have tried to become less abstract and to deal explicitly with the issue of formal content. We find it important to pursue and exploit the cultural connotations of the built world. As with our name, we prefer our work to arouse too many associations rather than too few. For us, buildings have come to represent a way of life, or ideas about a way of life, and this representation is specific. The vehicle chosen to represent or suggest a way of life is the building's subject. The architecture is then unabashedly obvious in its use of this subject. Rendered literally in the formal organisation of the building, the subject informs the planning as well as the imagery. . . Houses are castles, ranches, fairy tale cottages, Georgian townhouses, Spanish missions, etc. Chinese restaurants have Chinese facades. Las Vegas glitters and flashes like gold changing hands.

We are taught—as people with taste—to find this embarrassingly obvious. But an overabundance of tasteful restraint among architects has resulted in a phenomenally nondescript environment. Recently taste has been institutionalised in local design review boards. And taste, in Northern California, seems to be epitomised by one material: redwood. One colour—brown in all its various shades and forms from beige to dark bronze anodised—now dominates our landscape as the lowest common denominator of acceptable public taste. The Rustic Imperative, as we have experienced it in Northern California, is a holdover from a cultural movement so thoroughly assimilated that it is no longer recognisable. One might argue that as soon as redwood acquired the seal of good taste it lost its power to represent its particular way of life. . .

* * *

The El Rancho Rio Building, sited at the mouth of Carmel Valley, marks the confluence of two architectural styles which characterise much of the building on the Monterey Peninsula. Immediately to the west is the eighteenth-century Carmel Mission (Father Serra's favourite), an exceedingly picturesque adobe building, set in a semitropical landscape, owing equally to Baroque Spain and to Mexico. To the east is the nineteenth-century Larkin House (one of America's Hundred Finest Homes), the prototypical Monterey-style building. Its walls are also of adobe, but surrounded by deep wooden verandahs supported on slender columns, the whole intended by its builder, a transplanted New Englander, to recall the Greek Revival.

The El Rancho Rio is 'about' these two buildings. It makes careful appropriations from both in much the same way as these buildings appropriated from their sources. The outside is like the Larkin House, though rendered to simultaneously capture the public feeling of a boarded sidewalk in the Old West. Three connected courtyards—one for the cars, another for the entry, and a third for the fountain—are carved out of the interior.

Borrowing shapes and materials from the Carmel Mission, these courts also establish protected and serene interior spaces like those in their source.

In referring to well-known historical buildings, the El Rancho Rio refers also to the way of life they supported. It portrays the life possible in a modern office building whose occupants are permitted to emerge from their double-loaded corridors. Here they move instead through courtyards and along balconies and verandahs; they lunch on the base of the fountain; they work in their offices with French doors open wide to admit the mild climate. By recalling the built fabric that supported similar scenarios in an earlier time, we have tried to make a building that simultaneously reminds the occupants of that earlier way of life and permits them to re-enact the imagined scenarios. . .

In the El Rancho Rio, the locus of key scenarios is less tightly defined—the scenarios occur along the entire circulation system, though they cluster more densely about the entry lobby and the fountain court. So the resemblance to the subject is strongest in its covered verandahs, courtyards and balconies.

The trick, of course, is to find the right subject—one that captures the values of the clients as well as providing an imageable and fecund source for the design. We are extremely literal with our subjects, so we have to be convinced of them. We will not have the luxury of reinterpreting our designs. By eschewing the abstract, we make design rather difficult for ourselves. We do it this way for two reasons. First, because architecture is simply better when it is connected up with other types of experience, just as a building with history is better than the same building built today. And secondly, because we think that architecture is a much richer medium than its recent history has admitted. The tasteful abstractness characterising so much of our designed environment has established very limited expectations of what buildings may be concerned with. In other times and other places people have represented every facet of human existence in their buildings. We hope, through our pursuit of subject, to reclaim some of this abandoned territory as the legitimate domain of architecture.

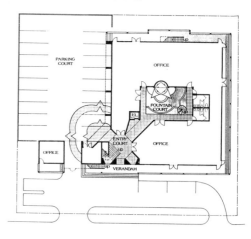

1 El Rancho Rio, plan at first floor. A frontally layered building with diagonal circulation focusing on a centre court.

2
3

4

2 El Rancho Rio, Carmel Valley, California, 1980. Verandah on the exterior for circulation is a traditional device of the area allowing a summer shade. (ph Rob Super)

3 Public entrance. (ph Rob Super)

4 Entry court. (ph Rob Super)

STANLEY TIGERMAN

Pensacola Place II Apartment Project, Chicago, Illinois, 1978–81

Dualistic Classicism

The harsh black and white imagery of the apartment slab underlines the dualism which Tigerman seeks in his recent work. Here two different modes—the Ionic and Miesian—are mingled and finally merged in a way which belies the strangeness of this act. In fact it appears almost natural. The flat Chicago frame is overlaid by a secondary order, the Ionic temple with a flat roof. The entablature hides the mechanical equipment, the balconies are engaged columns and the eroded black circles are volutes. The equation of housing with temple, an idea Ricardo Bofill is also testing, is more plausible than the equation of a house with machine, and it's an irony that Tigerman is here building his temple parallel to his previous mechanistic slab in the background. In both cases the perfect white grid of life encases an absolute black square of window, with its black anodised mullions. Tigerman, in his rather cryptic texts, speaks of these schemes as implying an infinite linear city and that form as entailing a dualism of death in life. Hence his lurid conceptual sketch of the scheme (see page 1).

Actually the group forms an interesting urban hybrid: part perimeter block raised on a deck, part shopping mall with townhouses, and part apartment slab. The mixed type is again superior in Tigerman's monolithic block of 1971–74 and gives a sense of domesticity, even if a diagrammatic one. What is Tigerman finally representing? The archetypal townhouse, the fundamental temenos for living in the city and, most quizically, the billboard temple—the oddity that balconies can become Ionic columns. This is hardly yet a humanism, or a serious representional programme, but it forms a pretext for a primitive ornament and urban discourse between types.

CJ

Page 1
Perspective of old (1971–4) and new schemes.
1 Conceptual drawing of the scheme as a linear city showing the dualism, the archetypal townhouse multiplied and the slab blocks *à redent*.
2 Perimeter block, plans.
3 View of West elevation, older scheme, 'Boardwalk' parallel to it, and Lake Shore Drive. (ph Howard N. Kaplan © HNK Architectural Photography)
4 East elevation, view of townhouses eroded into the surface, and the Miesian window wall above. (ph Howard N. Kaplan © HNK Architectural Photography)
5. West elevation shows a hexastyle temple with engaged Ionic columns and flared cyma recta cornice laid on top of a 26-bay Miesian grid. (ph Howard N. Kaplan © Architectural Photography)

1

2
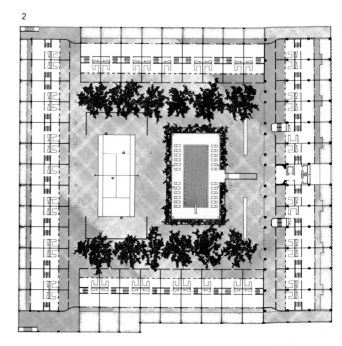

3

5

4

STANLEY TIGERMAN

The Anti-Cruelty Society, Chicago, Illinois, 1980–81

Ambivalent Classical Imagery

Stanley Tigerman's interest in dualism, as argued in his appropriately titled book Versus *(Rizzoli, 1982) can also be seen in this very humane Anti-Cruelty Society, a building with a dual purpose: it saves and rehabilitates stray dogs, but also has to dispose of them. This destructive/reconstructive opposition is conveyed in the drawings of the final project. The drawing of the elevation suggests a stark white temple with pediment, an affirmation of light and life, while the flat, horizontal factory image, industrial glazing and aluminium suggest, like the radioactive haze, a mechanical finality. Tigerman in his writing ('Post-Modernism is a Jewish Movement') dramatises ironies he finds in society, and here we can't escape the conclusion that he's making a comment on the 'final solution'. Thus several critics have seen the mocking dog face as an explicit piece of black humour. The popular song 'How much is that doggie in the window?' and its mindless sentimentality, are being satirised. And yet the architecture is dualistic and as ambivalent as any doubly-coded Post-Modernism.*

The visual cues are kept ambiguous, and are part of several systems of meaning. This keeps the representation from being too explicit or one-dimensional. Thus the dog's head (pediment), jowls (piano shapes) and mouth-tongue (Palladian door) are incorporated into abstract fenestration shapes—a continuous line of sash windows above, and shop windows below. This ambiguity is further reinforced by a mixture of domestic and institutional metaphors: a suburban residence is indicated by the conventional opposition between white trim and horizontal clapboard (actually in grey aluminium, but nonetheless looking like wood). Picket fence, interior blown-up dog kennel and other images of the home are set against an institutional, white Modernism—here the sign of an enlightened euthanasia. The plan and side elevation carry out this dualistic opposition between a classical idealism and a Modernist utilitarianism, a symmetry and opportunistic infill. *This combination represents a favourable evolution of an institution which is usually sheltered in tawdry and sentimental forms. That the office building can be a large house and the institution a partial home is a positive discovery (or rediscovery) of recent architects and social researchers.* CJ

The programme is a second-generation addition to a building originally designed in 1933 in 'Chicago World's Fair Moderne' with an addition in 1953, done in 'International Style modern'.

The original building(s) have tended to symbolise the more unpleasant aspects of the nature of the institution, ie, a euthanasia centre. The intention is to re-educate the public-at-large such that the euthanising aspect of the institution is diminished and the adaptive part of the programme is enhanced. Therefore the image of the new building is intended to suggest non-institutionality; residential imagery is suggested by the design which is thought of as apartments over a store.

The second floor of the addition is therefore fenestrated by double hung windows over storefront (the old 'doggie in the window' trick). The building is clad in horizontal aluminium siding, prefinished grey with white trim, having a Palladian cut-out, a key to a can of dogfood and the cheeks of a basset hound.

The original building's intrinsic architectural message was hermetically institutional; thus euthanising attitudes were supported. The Society wished to change that image, replacing it with a new one concerned with adoption; thus, semiotically speaking, the building is a sign—a billboard—that is intended to advertise the new message.

Stanley Tigerman

1 Main elevation, airbrush over mechanical drawing. The typical Post-Modern asymmetrical symmetry is underplayed for a stark, funereal monumentality. The Pop imagery is reinforced by the almost comic-strip drawing.

2

2 Main elevation. (ph Howard N Kaplan © HNK Architectural Photography)
3 Interior. Dog kennel image and picket fence treated as Pop icons are set against Modernist institutional white forms and ducts. (ph Howard N Kaplan © HNK Architectural Photography)
4 Lettering conceived as part of the formal system. (ph Howard N Kaplan © HNK Architectural Photography)

3

4

5 View showing domestic and factory images, the flat billboard facade and the background reality. The setbacks display the dogs for sale; the euthanasia facilities are in the rear. (ph Howard N Kaplan © HNK Architectural Photography)

6 Symmetrical ground floor plan with asymmetrical setbacks, a free plan of office elements and classical pavilions.

7 Upper floor plan; classicism and the open plan combined.

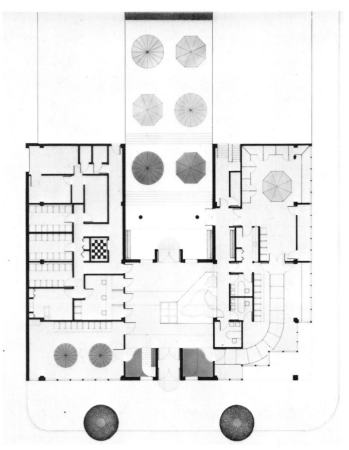

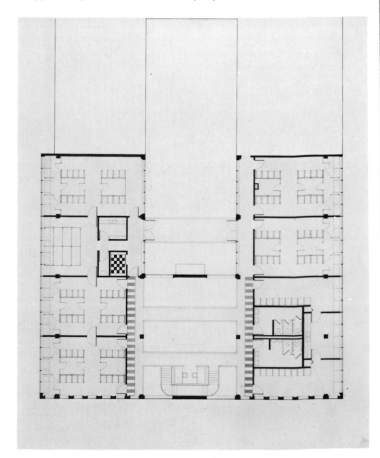

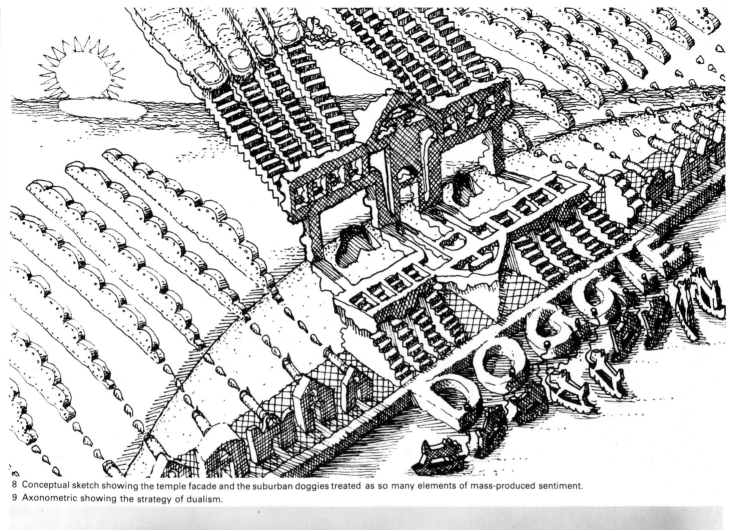

8 Conceptual sketch showing the temple facade and the suburban doggies treated as so many elements of mass-produced sentiment.
9 Axonometric showing the strategy of dualism.

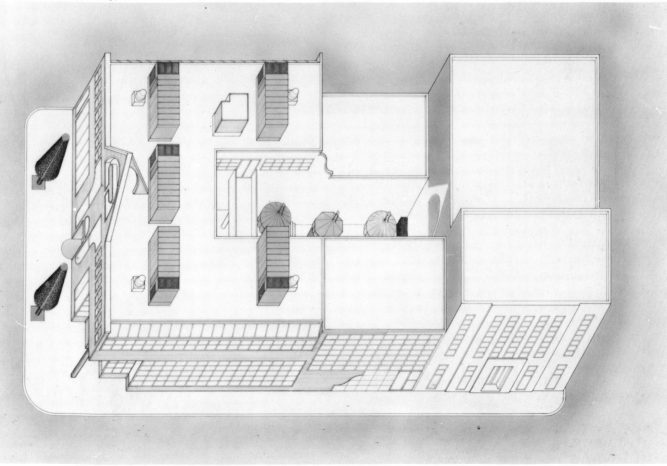

HELMUT JAHN

Four Towers, 1978–82

Representational Glass Towers

These four towers by Helmut Jahn show a cumulative development and a deepening understanding of the tall building as conceived within the possibilities of advanced glass technology. The glass and steel curtain wall is beginning to loose its totally abstract role and take on a flexible, if rather stiff, representational one. The tower is no longer the dumb box, although for economic reasons it may still have to be a heavy Skylump; it is no longer of a single colour, or simple shape and formula. Several contradictory elements now influence its design—the paramount one being symbolic imagery, at least on the outside. Jahn built three of these towers because they signified excellence, power and, quite openly, current fashion. Thus in the debate on abstraction vs representation they occupy a key place in the history of the recent skyscraper, because, along with Johnson's, Graves' and Pelli's notable buildings, they are among the first large Post-Modern constructions.

In my Skyscrapers, Skyprickers, Skycities *(1980) I argued that the history of the tall building could be seen as a substitution of metaphors across these, the three major types. A metaphor is a latent symbol which works most effectively when it is subliminal. Thus Jahn's Addition to the Chicago Board of Trade is an understated Mercedes, or Lincoln Continental, the answer to the Rolls Royce radiator of Philip Johnson, that potent architectural metaphor which has evolved from the Parthenon: the automobile imagery is present but veiled. The hard-edge material of two-tone glass clipped together by 'chrome' strips*

1 Chicago Board of Trade Addition, Chicago, 1978–82. A two-tone glass wall, and on the sides limestone screens, take up the Art Deco forms and stylise them on a rectangular grid. (ph Jahn/Murphy)

2 One South Wacker, Chicago, 1979–82. Silver square panels of glass enclose grey glass areas which divide the facade into three comprehensible parts. The fully polychromatic tower of glass, presaged by Robert Stern's Chicago Tribune entry (1980), has yet to be realised, but this is a step on the way. (ph Jahn/Murphy)

3 The skylump is lightened by the setbacks, central vertical section and shimmering glass. The 'light at night' drawings of Jahn recall the fireworks and light shows at Nuremburg, no doubt Albert Speer's best efforts as an architect.

4 Humana Project for Louisville, Kentucky, 1982. The Health Center *'crowns the building'* which is *'devoid of the starkness of the modern movement and without historicism and eclecticism'*—except of course a historicism of the recent past (see text). A wrap-around building was attempted by Pelli, but not, as here, based on helical growth.

5 Bank of the Southwest Tower, Houston, 1982-. Vertical, central grid set against horizontal sides, and a strong emphasis on the base and top. Corner entrances are set on the diagonal and celebrated by giant, eroded pediments.

6 The top-pitched roofs and spire, or beacon, resemble not only the bottom pediments but also some of the work of Frank Lloyd Wright. Note the octagonal form and the way this breaks the Houston grid; Johnson's Pennzoil is to the lower right.

7 Bank of the Southwest. Light divides the tower up into seven distinct levels.

1

2

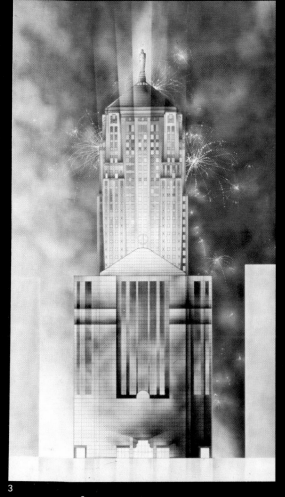

3

4

5

6

7

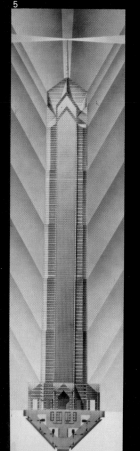

8

makes it a black Lincoln, while the radiator grill and hood emblem are also vaguely suggested. The fact that limestone sheathing is used on the sides, and the corners are chamfered to relate to the existing Art Deco building is perhaps clearer, and indeed this is the symbolism intended by Jahn. He also wished to represent the tripartite Skycolumn, with base, shaft and emphatic capital, and a generalised replica of the Board of Trade: 'The building derives its formal characteristics from an abstracted, literal duplication of the Art Deco style of the existing structure.' This idea of stylising glass to resemble masonry has been attempted by Philip Johnson in Pittsburgh, and it is a creative game when the details are reconceived in the new material. Here the building avoids pastiche, and the impossible contortions which may result from the translation. It's not a greatly inventive exercise, not a breakthrough, but important for Jahn's next exercise. . .

'One South Wacker', a raw-sounding name belonging to that Chicago tradition of pragmatic numbering and the memorialisation of money, uses the stagger and stepped form more effectively to break up the surface into discernible parts. Silver and grey glass form vertical 'columns' of area 10–15 storeys tall (they actually diminish towards the top). The building is articulated in plan to acknowledge a cross street and break up the mass. Again a base and capital are implied as in the equation of glass and masonry. But, as in the Chicago Board of Trade Addition the grid is used all over. This has the effect of reducing the building to the status of an industrial object which is made from a homogeneous material. The packaging may be ingenious, and we may marvel at the Slick Tech effects, but still ask for more by way of contrasts and meaning.

Jahn attempts greater complexities in his Humana Building— a competition for a tower won by Michael Graves. Jahn avers that he is representing the audacity of the corporation by a 'dramatic gesture' and 'dynamic curve'—the lift-off of the lower parts and the helical shape. We can see the influence of Tatlin's tower, Wright's Bartlesville and Johnson's Pennzoil as well as other Late-Modern experiments. With the beacon at the top— flashing out signs of good health for Humana (and its health club at the top)—there were obviously other references intended. But the scheme is notable as an exploration in mixing vertical typologies with spiral and horizontal ones.

The Bank of the Southwest for Houston, which won a competition in October 1982, combines several of these ideas in a true synthesis. The implied masonry and limestone screens have become real, or substantial, horizontal bands in places— around the base they are rusticated quoins and eroded pediments. Horizontal and vertical morphology are contrasted, as in the Humana project, giving more power to both. The volume diminishes in chamfered corners, as in the Chicago Board of Trade Addition, and the five 'columns' of glass are formed by staggered shapes and lights. The tripartite organisation is finally orchestrated and well proportioned: the fractured icebergs at the top not only finish the shaft with an emphatic sparkle, as they do at the Chrysler, but also culminate in a second crescendo, that of a beacon. This is clearly the skypricking hyperdermic needle of the Empire State Building. That the scheme is

8 Bank of the Southwest Tower, Houston, entrance. Rusticated bands and quoins focus on an eroded, simplified pediment, rather like a missing Ledoux.

9

well worked out geometrically—a rotated square and octagon—
and that its proportions relate well to an obelisk, may be due to
the luck of having a tight site (although it is not 'the most
slender tall building ever built'). But Jahn has understood the
possibilities of the site, programme and morphology and intended to symbolise them—proof if needed that we have re-
turned to the greater tradition of the Skyscraper/Skycity.
Representation, abstraction and technology are each given their
due.

CJ

The goals of the project are best expressed in the programme
statement by Century Development Corporation and the Bank
of the Southwest:
'The tower shall project an institutional, timeless character. It
should have a prominent architectural profile on the Houston
skyline. The architectural form should be distinctive and become a symbol of the project and its central presence in downtown Houston. The form of the base should express the strength
and substantial nature of a major banking institution and make
a major entry statement. The centrality of the site, particularly
with respect to its physical relationship to other major downtown towers and with respect to its potential as a focal point
for the Houston pedestrian tunnel system, should be expressed

9 Shreve, Lamb and Harmon, Empire State Building, New York, 1929–31. The
slender formula Jahn uses, with side setbacks and culminating needle. The Empire
State was also a Free Style Classical version of the tripartite, fluted column. (ph
Jencks)

in the architecture. This centrality also lends itself to the creation
of a major civic space. Material selection is extremely important
and should reflect both the institutional stature of the project
through the use of rich, traditional materials and current architectural expression through contemporary materials and
accents. Attention to detail throughout will be paramount in
defining and expressing project quality at all levels. Inherent in
the Bank's concept of institutionality and strength are certain
biases for three-dimensional or modulated exterior wall surfaces and against "glass wall architecture". The Bank's identity
should be established more through the building's importance
as an overall architectural statement than through its public
banking facilities within the building.'

The programme statement of the Bank of the Southwest
Tower recalls the Tribune Tower Competition of 1922. Here too,
the programme emphasised the formal, visual and symbolic
aspects over the technological and functional criteria, by calling
for 'the greatest building' in the world, evidently searching to
formulate a new typology and to explore the meaning of form—
an attempt certainly successful as we perceive it today.

These efforts to create a 'Historical Continuum' are represented in the design of the Bank of the Southwest Tower by
juxtaposing the spirit and richness of past forms and present-
day technique and materials.

The obelisk rotated on the site is the basic formal generator
of the design. Distinctively characteristic of the American landscape, monumental obelisks have been used to connote glory,
achievement and eternal duration. Besides many military connotations, the look-out platforms are indicative of the social
functions of these structures.

The corners of this tapered shaft gradually step back. All
surfaces terminate in a steep roof with spire and beacon—certainly reminiscent of the Chrysler Building—a 'top' for Houston,
representing the 'centrality' of the building.

The structural rationale in such a tall structure is economically
inescapable and intrinsically tied to the architecture of this
building, which is the most slender tall building ever built. In a
time when the framed and braced tube has become the
accepted solution to very tall structures, new technological and
structural limits are explored with an internally braced system
of two sets of 'superdiagonals' straddling the core in each direction. This 'Greek Cross' configuration transfers all gravity
loads to eight massive concrete columns, which provide the
stiffness for the structure. In plan, form and surface this structural configuration is of major influence on the architecture of
the building. Wind tunnel studies have also verified that the
shape of the overall tower, as well as the top and base, are of
great benefit in reducing the impact of the lateral forces on the
structure.

The materials on the tower combine the richness and quality
of the past with present-day possibilities in technology. The
twelve surfaces of the building's refined shape are treated in
different combinations of granite, aluminium or glass, to reinforce the shape, height and verticality of the building. Inherent
in the choice of these materials and their design is an effort to
project an institutional and timeless character with powerful
architectural impact. The gabled sides are aluminium and light
reflective glass with strong three-dimensional, vertical accen-
tuation. At the corners, glass alternates with two types of granite, with varying finishes and forms. The 'chamfers' are flush
silicone-glazed to emphasise its strength and solidity. The eight
columns are faced with stone and resolve with glass and metal
at the top.

Helmut Jahn

TAFT ARCHITECTS

Four Projects, Texas, 1978–82

Classical and Vernacular

These architects quite consciously set up an antithesis between a relaxed local language and the international Post-Modern Classicism. The antithesis also incorporates, quite traditionally, that ground between private and public, courtyard and figural gateway, utilitarian and symbolic, or the old set of distinctions between building and architecture. If it's an old game, it is nevertheless played here with a fresh appropriateness. Varied as the projects are from roadside architecture to townhouses and institutional buildings, the same set of concerns and language recur, but each time with a difference that is suitable to the task. Thus the Grove Court Townhouses suggest layered screens, as on a theatre stage, which provide increasing privacy in depth and height. The undulating stucco wall, a sign of informality and earth in all their work, is stepped and modulated to let the formal architecture rise above it in contrast. Erosion and figural shape signify the difference between the cirucmstancial and the ideal. In the particular language, the influence can be seen as a contrast between Robert Stern and Aldo Rossi, but no doubt the architects are well aware of the full tradition of Post-Modernism, and they do cite, in any case, Pre-Modern precedents.

Another interesting thread runs through their work, as in that of Michael Graves: the thin, layered facade as a sign of depth and density. Where economies do not allow a full sculptural modulation this density can be signified by trompe l'oeil of various kinds on a nearly flat skin. Conceptually, it is a curtain wall or membrane which is treated with different colours, grids, stucco, layers and shapes. All these provide the psychological equivalent of a richness that is absent, much the way the four Pompeian styles signifed an architecture that couldn't be afforded.

Finally, it is the transformation of urban typologies such as courtyard housing, or vernacular languages such as the Texan roadside, which gives this work a certain relaxed relevance. A team practice rarely provides such a consistent development of themes. CJ

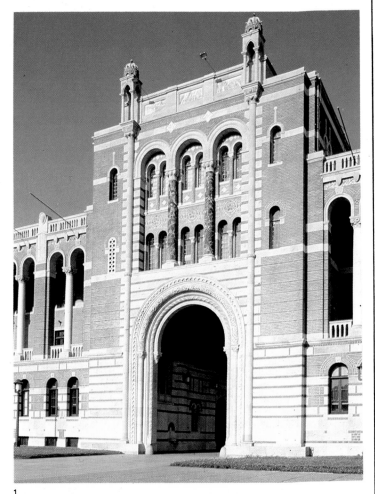

1

1 Cram Goodhue and Ferguson, Rice Campus, 1910. A relaxed Romanesque with a certain suitability to the climate and academic building task. James Stirling has recently transferred this vernacular, while Taft Architects treat it analogically. (ph Taft Architects)

2 Fat Franks Restaurant, Houston, Texas, 1979. 'Fat Franks' is a mythological trail cook who serves up chili, chicken fried steaks, speciality drinks and the usual Roadside-Wild-West-Fast-Food. The commercial and traditional vernaculars are so closely approximated that one might think this undesigned, until one approaches the corner and Venturi's 'decorated shed' is revealed. Stepped forms, wandering dado levels and scale distortions on an implied gable front are recurrent elements in Taft's work. (ph Taft Architects)

3 Commonwealth Townhouses, Houston, Texas, 1981. Like Inigo Jones' Wilton House, to which this scheme explicitly relates, corner pavilions define a public edge which contrasts with a more domestic inner courtyard. The busy streets on which the townhouses are located also have a grand formality although not, as here, contrasted with an informal, stuccoed base. (ph Taft Architects)

4 Catholic Student Center, Houston, Texas, 1980. Archetypal and abstract forms are eroded and combined in different materials—brick, tile, gridded stucco, concrete tile roof and aluminium—to set up again an opposition between formal and informal, architecture and building. The precedent is Eliel Saarinen's Cranbrook Academy. (ph Taft Architects)

2

5 Grove Court Townhouses, Houston, Texas, 1978–81. A vernacular of wood frame, gypsum board and stucco is the background for this low-cost housing. Like the courtyard housing of Irving Gill from which it is derived, very simple and subtle means blend together existing trees, private gardens and public space. Tile and porthole suggest an order without naming it. (ph Taft Architects)

3

4

5

Taft Architects

The work of Taft Architects is a collective effort of the three partners, John J Casbarian, Danny Samuels, and Robert H Timme. Two important aspects characterise this work: the design process and circumstantial issues deemed important.

The design process is one that fosters exploration, with the result that the work is divergent in character. The process generates various 'pure' schemes and incorporates their strengths into a complex design. This is, in effect, an acceptance of the fact that an environment may simultaneously have multiple readings

The second aspect is based on the tradition of finding in the problem the concerns that shape the design. These include the context, the relationship of the activities; the desires of the client; and the practicalities of construction and budget.

There are also architectural concerns. These include issues of scale, material, craft and colour. Many of these issues are, in fact, rediscoveries of concerns which have always been a part of architecture, but were, through the Modern Movement, redirected or even lost.

The basis for the initiation of this direction owes much to our early experiences at Rice University and in Houston, Texas during the 1960s. The foundation studio at the School of Architecture, in the tradition of the Bauhaus, provided us with an abstract conceptual process for exploring two- and three-dimensional structures. Later at Rice, and afterwards, we worked with teachers from the Saarinen tradition. The emphasis was on making rational decisions within a comprehensive conceptual framework, finding within the problem itself the concerns that shape its solution. Three-dimensional investigation and exploration, through modelling at various scales, were important aspects of this process. From these experiences we developed a belief that clear, abstract ordering systems can sustain themselves, accommodate, and become enriched by detailed development.

Almost unremarked at first, but growing in importance for us, was the Rice Campus itself, by Cram Goodhue and Ferguson. Finding in Houston, in 1910, no tangible architectural context, they invented an appropriate, hot-climate, Gothic style, almost Venetian in scale, texture, and colour. However stylistically fanciful, careful attention was given to climatic responsiveness. Thin buildings allowed cross-ventilation, while deep arcades provided protection from heavy rain and intense sun.

Our work does not refer directly to history, but rather has to do with continuity of issues and appropriateness of attitudes. We are more interested in reinterpretation than accurate reconstruction. We are, however, drawn to examples of work from architectural history in which two sets of seemingly conflicting concerns coexist, allowing aspects of each position to occur at various scales.

In our own work an illustration of this attitude is evident in Grove Court Townhouses (1978), in Houston. The project combines functionalist, loft-like volumes with a layered ordering system, thereby delineating a hierarchy of public to private spaces. The play of undulating planes set against the gridded volumes are reminiscent of Mackintosh. As in Bella Vista Terrace Apartments, by Irving Gill, a minimal distinction is established between indoor and outdoor spaces.

Two projects, The Municipal Control Building (1978), in Missouri City, and Fat Franks Restaurant (1979), in Houston, each employ an overscaled planar facade, abstractly representative of the building type. In the Control Building, the scale and proportion are similar to Ledoux's Gate Houses and to WPA public buildings of the 1930s. In the restaurant, the plane evokes the image of early Texas commercial street-front architecture.

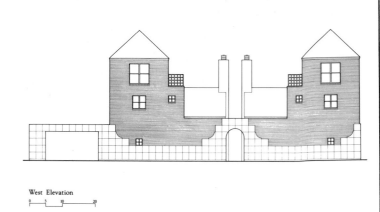

West Elevation

0   5   10   20

6

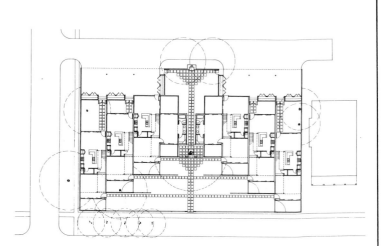

1st. Floor Site Plan

0   10   20   30

7
8

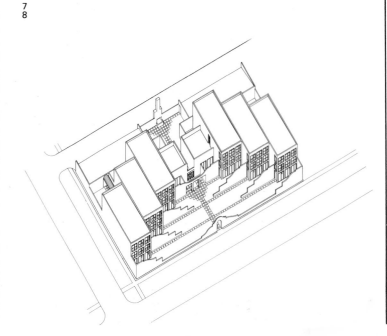

In the YWCA Masterson Branch (1979), in Houston, a clearly functionalist (Modernist) plan is overlaid with a visual ordering system, describing various readings of scale and marking entrances. The main entrance to the YWCA evokes a resemblance to the Sallyport in Lovett Hall, the main administration building at Rice, by Cram Goodhue and Ferguson, not so much in form, but in symbolic intent. The Sallyport marks the threshold to the academic environment beyond; the YWCA entrance is a gateway to both the communal activities within, and the recreational park beyond. On the interior, the celebration of the industrial character of the fixtures (overhead doors, sodium vapour lights, return air grilles) reflects the attitude, rather than the specific

6 Commonwealth Townhouses, west elevation. Two of the four houses rise with an asymmetrical symmetry behind the gridded stucco; the private gardens can be sensed in back, indicated by trellis and informal composition. Rossi and Venturi have used the square window and pavilion in similar ways.
7, 8 Grove Court Townhouses, plan and axonometric. Semi-private and shared garden interpenetrate in front, while a giant, Texas barbecue unites the group as a focus in back.

9 Grove Court Townhouses, entrance gate. The gentle curves, reminiscent of Mission Style, swell up one behind another to layer space as a series of theatre screens. (ph Taft Architects)

9

solution, taken by Otto Wagner in his Vienna Postal Savings Bank.

The Catholic Student Center (1980), in Houston, establishes an outdoor central space, almost Byzantine in character, surrounded by functional activity areas. As in Saarinen's work, the reinterpretation of the context and the programme enables the building to take on new meanings, while maintaining references to its neighbourhood context and to earlier religious antecedents.

The Talbot House (1980), in Nevis, employs a Palladian organisational system, inherent in the British colonial architectural influence on the island. It is, perhaps, more a contextual response, rather than a specific historic reference. Moreover, such an order was suggested in the desire of the clients for a central, public, communal space from which private spaces are reached, for the purpose of reinforcing a sense of family. Natural ventilation can be accommodated by this symmetrical plan, since breezes on the site vary in direction.

Commonwealth Townhouses (1981), in Houston, are organised with an inward focus, creating a cool, enclave-like environment. Although the volumetric disposition is clearly Palladian, the scale and single-image identity of Commonwealth are more reflective of the context, an area of old stately mansions.

John J Casbarian, Danny Samuels, Robert H Timme

TAFT ARCHITECTS
YWCA Masterson Branch, Houston, Texas, 1980-82

1 *Serliana* marks the public entrance for women, and its steps and curves break into the grids above.

2 Undulating and wiggly ramp leads to the gym and pool. Blue grills for air ducts or sound absorbing tiles have a Secessionist and Sternesque flavour.
All phs Taft Architects

3 View of the 350-foot wall which looks north onto the parking lot. Steps and materials break the heaviness, while classical motifs announce each entrance.

4 Stepped forms flare out and the blue-and-white bands graduate upwards to metaphorically lighten the light-filled gymnasium: a healthy place to work out, rather like Le Corbusier's symbolic imagery of the 1920s.

Fragmented Classicism

Various well-known classical motifs are abstracted, amplified and distorted on this 350-foot facade, virtually a long window-less wall. The wall itself steps up and down and gives the impression of stepping in and out due to the different layered materials. Public symbolism is the keynote. The two main entrances are surmounted by blown-up, flat-arch shapes: for the female public to the left there is the Serliana, with stepped edges, and for the office workers, to the right, an oculus window over a 'cathedral' door staggered in plan. Children and their mothers enter the day-care centre through a small, Mission-Style arch.

The colour and material, also fragmented in layers, support these subtle semantic distinctions. Thus terracotta tile, unifying the base like a brown, rusticated basement, gives a ceremonial weight to the whole wall, in effect marking it as the public facade; but then this material climbs up to the right end and merges with the terracotta brown paint, around the back, to indicate the office area. Cream stucco with its scored grid and grey stucco with blue tile stripes, further fragment and lighten the heavy wall. Like the work of Michael Graves, from which it stems, this fragmented layering represents earth, architecture and sky. More particularly, the omnipresent blue represents the well-known blue triangle of the YWCA. Indeed, the colour harmonies and recurrent blues and gridded shapes make the addition of lettering seem to be an inevitable decoration. Rarely are words successfully incorporated into modern architecture.

If the abstract, classical forms recall many precedents without naming them, they also relate to current preoccupations: the Bill-Ding-Board Building of Robert Venturi and the Secessionist grids revived by Stern and Graves. In this sense, Taft is developing some of the conventions of the Post-Modern language, and relating them to the Texas vernacular, particularly the false-front store.

As an overall image for the YWCA, the building achieves a successful opposition between a bright and healthy informality and a formal institution. The stepping wall and its symbolism provide an urban facade suitable to the modest role of the health club while the fragmented volumes in back relate to the landscape and view. Classical front, picturesque behind is one antinomy supported by the Modernist open plan set against the closed room. The most important space, the multi-purpose room, is skewed in plan. All things considered this is a friendly, modest institution.

CJ

The brief was to provide a new YWCA downtown branch and central administrative facility, consisting of day-care centre, classrooms, crafts room, racquet ball court, locker rooms, offices, swimming pool (to be enclosed at a later stage), and multi-purpose room. The central administrative facility functions separately, and requires distinct identification. YWCA desired a strong and fresh image for the entire facility.

Located at the intersection of major arteries, surrounded by a transitional neighbourhood of mixed use—old houses, mid-rise commercial and industrial structures—the irregular-shaped site overlooks a city park.

The solution is conceived as a linear service structure, 350 feet long, containing the single-storey functions of offices, class-rooms and lockers, stacked on two floors, linked to two pavilions—a multi-purpose room and a pool complex. An indoor

5
6

5 Internal mouldings, in a Sternesque Gothic manner, mark important niches and unimportant drinking fountains. (ph Taft Architects)
6 Layered Post-Modern space with the volumes accentuated by colour. (ph Taft Architects)

plaza with central ramp provides major definition of place within the building, serving also as overflow for activities around it. Overhead doors provide flexibility in use of the multi-purpose room and plaza. Colour, texture and pattern are used for scale definition. Entrance to different activities are celebrated and given structural notice. Blue tile trim refers to the Blue Triangle, the original name and graphic identity of the YWCA. Handicapped access to all spaces is provided by ramps and bridges between structures. These spaces become exciting galleries for viewing activities.

The YWCA presents an image of a gateway to new experiences of the community, and the central space within is truly a mixed area for all the activities of community concern.

Taft Architects

7 Longitudinal section.
8 Ground floor plan with the skewed multi-purpose room.
9 First floor plan mixes the open and closed plans.
10 Perspective.

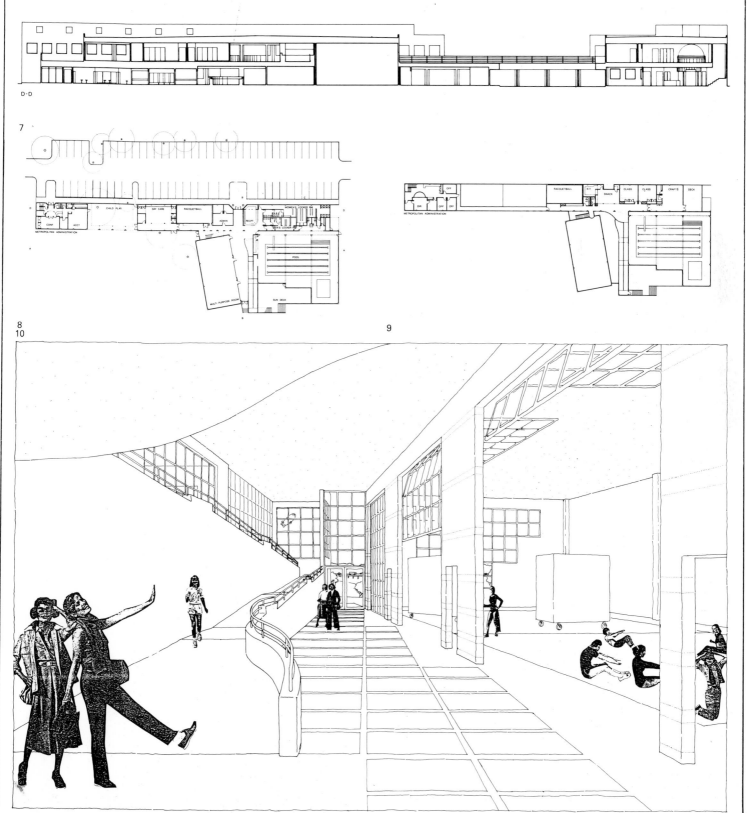

TAFT ARCHITECTS

Talbot House, Nevis, West Indies, 1980–81

Polychromatic Palladianism

This villa in the West Indies is an incredibly cheap version of a grand building type—a $32 per square foot version of the Villa Rotonda. The Palladian plan is the typical nine square problem focused on a central living space which opens out to four decks. Because of the climate, this house can be much more open than its usual masonry counterpart; because of the traditional styles in the area the bright colours can be expected: dark red roofs, light blues and creams.

In fact the house is a very interesting mixture of types: Venetian palace and centralised church. Instead of the central dome there is a pyramidal ceiling oriented to the four horizons. This motif is taken up in the four corner pavilions and emphasised, in every case, by cross-bracing that also points to the four views. Three of the four pavilions are for sleeping, the fourth is a kitchen, and all of them are painted pairs of complementary colours. Different floral motifs are stylised in a geometrical pattern, based on the triangle, and then stencilled in a way that recalls the ornament of Alexander 'Greek' Thomson. CJ

The programme was to provide a residence for a Vermont maple syrup farmer, his wife and child, on Nevis, where they planned to cultivate citrus fruit. Nevis is a small volcanic island in the Lesser Antilles. Buildings on the island are constructed from cut native stone and wood, and painted in complementary colours. Roofs are either red or green, which culturally are felt to be neighbourly colours. The massing of the buildings is formal in organisation. The main influence on the architecture is clearly the British colonisation of the island.

The house is located on the former site of the main house of Jessups Plantation. The site is half way up Nevis Peak overlooking the Caribbean Sea, on axis with a stately mango tree and cistern from the original plantation.

The house is conceived as four cut stone two-storey structures that define a central pavilion. The spaces between the stone structures form four terraces. The ground floors of the stone structures serve as garages and workrooms. A 35,000-gallon cistern is located below the central living pavilion. On the second, or main, level, three of the stone buildings are bedrooms and the fourth is the kitchen. The cut stone for the house was found on the site, probably used in earlier structures and garden walls.

The organisation allows for exterior exposure in all directions. This factor, coupled with the design of the oversized casement windows, allows for cross ventilation in all spaces, regardless of breeze direction, which is variable on the island. The house has no electricity; power for lighting, food preparation and refrigeration is provided by kerosene. A major concern in the development of the organisation was the relationship of the private spaces in the stone structures to the public area in the main pavilion. A sense of family structure is imparted by having to move into the family space prior to entering private areas.

The exterior wood is painted complementary red-orange and blue-green; lighter values used on the stone structures, darker values for the central pavilion. On the interior, each room is painted in a different pair of complementary colours. Bands of floral patterns are hand-stencilled at the top of each room.

Taft Architects

1 Grand staircase opens to the west and view; master bedroom to the left; kitchen to the right. Cut stone from the site forms the suggestion of a rusticated base; the dark centre living space emphasises the side pavilions. (ph Taft Architects)

2 Central living room with its roof truss and kerosene chandelier even picking up the four horizons; note the openness to the outside and the way this is represented in the floral ornament. (ph Taft Architects)

ABSTRACT
REPRESENTATION

Michael Graves, *Environmental Education Center*, Liberty State Park, New Jersey, 1980–83. This wildlife teaching center abstracts the representational images of the area—indeed their material as well as shape—into a series of pavilions with views of the flora and fauna, the gate, pediment and aedicule; more abstract architectural images are also represented. (ph Proto Acme Photo)

Michael Graves

A Case for Figurative Architecture

A *standard form* and a *poetic form* exist in any language or in any art. Although analogies drawn between one cultural form and another prove somewhat difficult, they nevertheless allow associations that would otherwise be impossible. Literature is the cultural form which most obviously takes advantage of standard and poetic usages, and so may stand as a model for architectural dialogue. In literature, the standard, accessible, simple ranges of daily use are expressed in conversational or prose forms, while the poetic attitudes of language are used to test, deny and, at times, to further support standard language. It seems that standard language and poetic language have a reciprocal responsibility to stand as separate and equal strands of the greater literary form and to reinforce each other by their similarity and diversity. Through this relationship of tension, each form is held in check and plays on the other for its strength.

When applying this distinction of language to architecture, it could be said that the standard form of building is its common or internal language. The term 'internal language' does not imply in this case that it is inaccessible, but rather that it is intrinsic to building in its most basic form—determined by pragmatic, constructional, and technical requirements. In contrast, the poetic form of architecture is responsive to issues external to the building, and incorporates the three-dimensional expression of the myths and rituals of society. Poetic forms in architecture are sensitive to the figurative, associative, and anthropomorphic attitudes of a culture. If one's goal is to build with only utility in mind, then it is enough to be conscious of technical criteria alone. However, once aware of and responsive to the possible cultural influences on building, it is important that society's patterns of ritual be registered in the architecture. Could these two attitudes, one technical and utilitarian and the other cultural and symbolic, be thought of as architecture's standard and poetic languages?

Without doubt, the inevitable overlap of these two systems of thought can cause this argument to become somewhat equivocal. However, the salient tendencies of each attitude may be distinguished and reasonably discussed. This is said with some critical knowledge of the recent past. It could be maintained that dominant aspects of Modern architecture were formulated without this debate about standard and poetic language, or internal and external manifestations of architectural culture. The Modern Movement based itself largely on technical expression—internal language—and the metaphor of the machine dominated its building form. In its rejection of the human or anthropomorphic representation of previous architecture, the Modern Movement undermined the poetic form in favour of non-figural, abstract geometries. These abstract geometries might in part have been derived from the simple internal forms of machines themselves. Coincident with machine metaphors in buildings, architecture in the first half of this century also embraced aesthetic abstraction in general. This has contributed to our interest in purposeful ambiguity, the possibility of double readings within compositions.

While any architectural language, to be built, will always exist within the technical realm, it is important to keep the technical expression parallel to an equal and complementary expression of ritual and symbol. It could be argued that the Modern Movement did this, that as well as its internal language it expressed the symbol of the machine, and therefore practised cultural symbolism. But in this case, the machine is retroactive, for the machine itself is a utility. So this symbol is not an external allusion, but rather a second, internalised reading. A significant architecture must incorporate both internal and external expressions. The external language, which engages inventions of culture at large, is rooted in a figurative associational and anthropomorphic attitude.

We assume that in any construct, architectural or otherwise, technique, the art of making something, will always play its role. However, it should also be said that the components of architecture are not only derived from pragmatic necessity, but have also evolved from symbolic sources. Architectural elements are recognised for their symbolic aspect and used metaphorically by other disciplines. A novelist, for example, will stand his character next to a window and use the window as a frame through which we read or understand the character's attitude and position.

In architecture, however, where they are attendant to physical structure, basic elements are more frequently taken for granted. In this context, the elements can become so familiar that they are not missed when they are eliminated or when they are used in a slang version. For instance, if we imagine ourselves standing adjacent to a window, we expect the window-sill to be somehow coincident with the waist of our body. We also expect, or might reasonably ask, that its frame help us make sense not only of the landscape beyond, but also of our own position relative to the geometry of the window and to the building as a whole. In modern architecture, however, these expectations are seldom met, and instead the window is often continuous with the wall as horizontal banding or, more alarmingly, it becomes the entire surface. The naming of the 'window wall' is a prime example of the conflation or confusion of architectural elements.

Architectural elements require this distinction, one from another, in much the same way as language requires syntax: without variations among architectural elements, we will lose the anthropomorphic or figurative meaning. The elements of any enclosure include wall, floor, ceiling, column, door, and window. It might be wondered why these elements, given their geometric similarity in some cases (for example, floor and ceiling) must be understood differently. It is essential in any symbolic construct to identify the thematic differences between various parts of the whole. If the floor as ground is regarded as distinct from the soffit as sky, then the material, textural, chromatic, and decorative inferences are dramatically different. Yet in a formal sense, these are both horizontal planes.

We as architects must be aware of the difficulties and the strengths of thematic and figural aspects of the work. If the external aspects of the composition, that part of our language which extends beyond internal, technical requirements, can be thought of as the resonance of man and nature, we quickly sense a historical pattern of external language. All architecture before the Modern Movement sought to elaborate the themes of man and landscape. Understanding the building involves both association with natural phenomena (for example, the ground is like the floor), and anthropomorphic allusions (for example, a column is like a man). These two attitudes within the symbolic nature of building were probably originally in part ways of justifying the elements of architecture in a pre-scientific society. However, even today, the same metaphors are required for access to our own myths and rituals within the building narrative.

Although there are, of course, instances where the technical assemblage of buildings employs metaphors and forms from nature, there is also the possibility of a larger, external natural text within the building narrative. The suggestion that the soffit is in some sense celestial is certainly our cultural invention, and it becomes increasingly interesting as other elements of the building also reinforce such a narrative. This type of cultural association allows us 'into' the full text or language of the architecture. This is in contrast to modern examples which commonly sacrifice the idea or theme in favour of a more abstract language. In these instances, the composition, while perhaps formally satisfying, is based only on internal references. A De Stijl composition is as satisfying turned upside down as it is right side up, and this is in part where its interest lies. We may admire it for its compositional unity, but as architecture, because of its lack of interest in nature and gravity, it dwells outside the reference systems of architectural themes. A De Stijl building has two internal systems, one technical and the other abstract.

In making a case for figurative architecture, we assume that the thematic character of the work is grounded in nature and is simultaneously read in a totemic or anthropomorphic manner. An example of this double reading might be had by analysing the character of a wall. As the window helps us to understand our size and presence within the room, so the wall, though more abstract as a geometric plane, has over time accommodated both pragmatic and symbolic divisions. Once the wainscot or chair rail is understood as being similar in height to the window-sill, associations between the base of the wall (which that division provides) and our own bodies are easily made. As we stand upright and are, in a sense, rooted in the ground, so the wall, through its wainscot division, is rooted relative to the floor. Another horizontal division takes place at the picture moulding, where the soffit is dropped from its horizontal position to a linear division at the upper reaches of the wall. Although this tripartite division of the wall into base, body, and head does not literally imitate man, it nevertheless stabilises the wall relative to the room, an effect we take for granted in our bodily presence there.

The mimetic character that a wall offers the room, as the basic substance of its enclosure, is obviously distinct from the plan of the room. While we see and understand the wall in a face-to-face manner, we stand perpendicular to the plan. The wall contributes primarily to the character of the room because of its figurative possibilities. The plan, however, because it is seen perspectively, is less capable of expressing character and more involved with our spatial understanding of the room. While space can be appreciated on its own terms as amorphous, it is ultimately desirable to create a reciprocity between wall and plan, where the wall surfaces or enclosures are drawn taut around a spatial idea. The reciprocity of plan and wall is finally more interesting than the distinctions between them.

We can say that both wall and plan have a centre and edges. The plan alone, however, has no top, middle and base, as does the wall. At this point, we must rely on the reciprocal action or volumetric continuity provided by both. Understanding that it is the volumetric idea that will ultimately be considered, we can analyse, with some isolation, how the plan itself contributes to

a figurative architectural language.

For the purposes of this argument, a linear plan, three times as long as it is wide, might be compared to a square or centroidal plan. The square plan provides an obvious centre, and at the same time, emphasises its edges or periphery. If the square plan is further divided, as in hop-scotch, into nine squares, the result is an even greater definition of corners, edges, and a single centre. If we continue to elaborate such a geometric proposition with free-standing artifacts such as furniture, the locations of tables and chairs will be not only pragmatic, but also symbolic of societal interactions. One can envisage many compositions and configurations of the same pieces of furniture which would offer us different meanings within the room.

Predictably, the three-square composition will subdivide quite differently from the centroidal plan. While the rectangular composition will distinguish the middle third of the room as its centre, and the outer thirds as its flanks, we are less conscious here of occupiable corners. The corners of the square composition contribute to our understanding of the centre and are read as positive. In contrast, the corners of the rectangular plan are remote from its centre and are seemingly residual. Our culture understands the geometric centre as special and as the place of primary human occupation. We would not typically divide the rectangular room into two halves, but rather, more appropriately, would tend to place ourselves in the centre, thereby precluding any reading of the room as a diptych. In analysing room configurations, we sense a cultural bias to certain basic geometries. We habitually see ourselves, if not at the centre of our 'universe', at least at the centre of the spaces we occupy. This assumption colours our understanding of the differences between centre and edge.

If we compare the understanding of the exterior of the building to that of its interior volume, another dimension of figurative architecture arises. A free-standing building such as Palladio's Villa Rotonda, is comprehensible in its objecthood. Furthermore, its interior volume can be read similarly—not as a figural object, but as a figural void. A comparison between such an 'object building' and a building of the Modern Movement, such as Mies van der Rohe's Barcelona Pavilion, allows us to see how the abstract character of space in Mies' building dissolves any reference to or understanding of figural void or space. We cannot charge Mies with failing to offer us figurative architecture, for this is clearly not his intention. However, we can say that, without the sense of enclosure that the Palladio example offers us, we have a much thinner pallette than if we allow the possibility of both the ephemeral space of modern architecture and the enclosure of traditional architecture. It could be contended that amorphic or continuous space, as understood in the Barcelona Pavilion, is oblivious to bodily or totemic reference, and we therefore always find ourselves unable to feel centred in such space. This lack of figural reference ultimately contributes to a feeling of alienation in buildings based on such singular propositions.

In this discussion of wall and plan, an argument is made for the figural necessity of each particular element and, by extension, of architecture as a whole. While certain monuments of the Modern Movement have introduced new spatial configurations, the cumulative effect of non-figurative architecture is the dismemberment of our former cultural language of architecture. This is not so much a historical problem as it is one of a cultural continuum. It may be glib to suggest that the Modern Movement be seen not so much as a historical break but as an appendage to the basic and continuing figurative mode of expression. However, it is nevertheless crucial that we re-establish the thematic associations invented by our culture in order to allow the culture of architecture to represent fully the mythic and ritual aspirations of society.

99

MICHAEL GRAVES

Humana Medical Corporation Headquarters, Louisville, Kentucky, 1982–86

Eclectic Classicism

Michael Graves' winning entry in yet another competition is this 27-storey skyscraper, due to be completed in 1986 at a cost of 45 million dollars. Other competitors included Norman Foster, Ulrich Franzen, Cesar Pelli and Helmut Jahn. Graves' scheme for the medical corporation Humana is almost a pun on its name: the 'humanism' is not only in the knowing re-use of the classics, but also in the celebration of the human body. A strong facade faces Main Street, with forehead, mouth and eyes. This face also holds the main health facilities—the exercise rooms and squash courts, the look-out post cantilevered out on a steel truss, and the sauna and pools. If 'health' is in the head, then the offices are in the body and the public, commercial facilities occupy the legs. This tripartite organisation is clear, although the anthropomorphic metaphors are kept abstract, and multivalent.

The overall body image, for instance, is oriented sharply to the view of the Ohio River: belvedere, curve and pediment see to that. But if one explores this body further it allows several opposite readings besides the human one. There is an L-shape organisation (typical of many 1930s New York skyscrapers) that places emphasis on the lower front, and turns the overall shape into an up-ended animal; the centipede top runs at right angles to this and several 'backbones' of glass indicate circulation. If all this zoomorphism sounds fanciful, it is because Graves veils, or abstracts, the sources and combines them with others.

As to the eclecticism of references, there is no doubt. The cantilevered truss of Lissitsky, used previously in an honorific

1 Model viewed from Main Street. The lower block 'temple' forms the entrance, holds the street-line and, at the top, contains executive offices which overlook a terrace. (ph Proto Acme Photo, Princeton NJ)
2 Preliminary studies showing the massing towards Main Street and the Ohio River, the idea of bringing the street into a curved waterfall, and the stepped volumes. There are also experiments with square windows, towers, cantilevers, the barrel vault as void and the elision of surfaces. Other sketches explored elements of a classical and vernacular vocabulary.

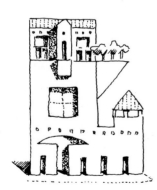

MAIN

OHIO RIVER

2

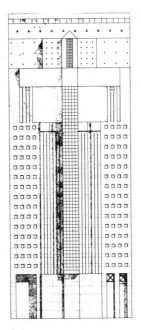
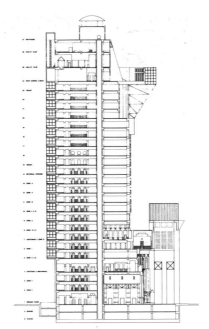
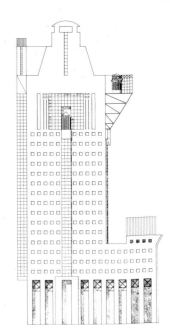

3, 4, 5 South elevation, section and Fifth Street elevation. The abstract archetypal nature of the fabric is evident in the repetition of squares. Variation from these gives added significance to what are, otherwise, normal classical shapes: the Roman grill, a Hoffmann temple, the truss and barrel vault.

way to display Lenin, is used here to recall the exposed trusses of the Ohio bridges, and holds a small blue 'cabanon'—the aedicules of Le Corbusier and Aldo Rossi. In even this single, functional icon are embedded four heterogeneous memories.

The top and base slots of space are based on Boullée's 'architecture of shadows', but they obviously also relate to other more current images: the base piers are like those of Johnson's AT&T, a forest of high pylons, a hypostyle hall meant to draw in the public while also holding the street line. In fact Graves has simply reversed the AT&T, pulling the back arcade to the front to make the front less imposing. At the top, repeated deep slots are placed at an angle, recalling the hydroelectric dams of the South. At the very top, the 'architecture of shadows' is again transformed, now into a vernacular image à la Krier, to recapitulate the two previous themes. This kind of transformation and recapitulation was, of course, the typical rhetorical trope of the Egyptian column, as well as the old American skyscraper. Thus memories are again heterogeneous.

The use of three main colours underscores this divergence. The cool pastel blue, cream and rust are in the typical Graves pallette (now something of a convention in America) but they also relate to the colours of the south-west—the adobe of New Mexico. In blue grass Kentucky they may appear slightly exotic, especially next to the glass and steel curtain walls, but even the machine aesthetic is incorporated slightly in the flat concrete walls, hard glass areas and exposed truss. Colour also relates to locale—the creamy-orange Kesota limestone is native to the region—and to function in that the reddish granite bands the giant entrance and frames the piers. In Graves' work red is often equated with the earth, blue with sky and cream with background. At Portland the formula was similar, although red was used in the 'shoulder' keystone and black at the base.

What makes Graves' eclecticism convincing, here as in his other work, is its transformational power. Sources are not entirely recognisable, nor are they obliterated; rather they remain in partial focus, pulled into a synthetic vision. This process of assimilation can be seen in the small conceptual sketches. Building types are merged into the basic low/high configuration, the setback necessitated by site and view. In some sketches an arcade, temple and tower morphology are mixed in the base; a giant square window, recessed void and concrete wall (as at Portland) are tried out in the shaft; experiments with pyramid,

linear barn, gable, and Greek Cross cathedral are made for the top. Several recurrent motifs such as the barrel vault and angled cantilever are switched around—to end up in different places in the final design. Throughout the process is the Gravesian aesthetic: the volumetric pencil line which outlines the basic classical shapes and gives them a modelling shade; the elision of surfaces across volumes (low and high); the sectional expression (the cut-off barrel vault); the archetypal elements (the vernacular classicism).

Graves' ability to go from strength to strength, winning ever-larger competitions without a diminution of control, must be the envy of every large practice. He has graduated from back-porch design to skyscrapers without losing conviction and this must stem, in part, from his intellectual background as a member of the New York Five, as well as from his ability to sketch and paint. The combination of the opposed qualities of artist, intellectual and organiser is rare in American architecture and one has to return to the example of H H Richardson to find a comparable figure—in quality, success, and perhaps even in a similar Free Style Classicism.

CJ

In accord with Humana's interest in recognising the unique character of the Louisville site, we have taken the presence of the Ohio River and an understanding of both the specific and general urban context as two primary influences on the design of our building. Our design addresses the river and the city, not only in terms of the views that they offer, but also for the thematic associations they suggest. The formal gestures and activities of our building are, we believe, natural and intrinsic to urban structure in general and a river city in particular. In their figurative and thematic aspect they attempt to reaffirm and re-establish humanist aspirations for the city which have been too long neglected by modern architecture.

With the onset of the Modern Movement in architecture, the prevailing humanist code based on the representation of man and landscape was supplanted by new technical interests born out of the Industrial Revolution. This technical aesthetic or machine metaphor inspired today's steel and reflective glass towers and their minimalist configurations, structures which, with some hindsight, we now recognise as being anti-urban and alienating to the human spirit. With the Modernist trend, the

6

7
9

6, 7 Model from north-east (Main Street) and west. The low portion holds the streetline, the tall part holds the skyscraper line and doesn't dwarf the street. The tall front door is reminiscent of both Le Corbusier's Chandigarh and the recent work of Ricardo Bofill. The profile is somewhat like the Vesnins' Pravda Building of 1923 and other Constructivist work of the Romantic Classicists at that time.

8 Site plan showing two main entrances focusing, above, on the curved waterfall and lobby and, right, from Fifth Avenue, on the elevator core.

9 Entry from public loggia with fountains to either side of portal. The ornament and figural shapes are aetiolated in a thirties stripped classical manner.

8

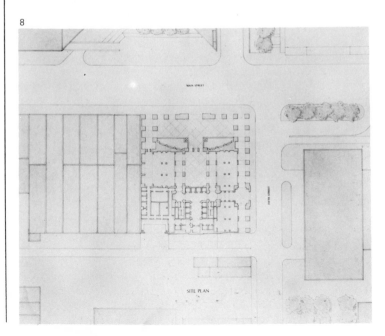

individual's ability to identify with his place, whether it be the city as a whole or an office within the building, has been dramatically diminished. Responsible urban architecture today must try to counteract this unfortunate effect.

Any attempt to develop Humana's new building site must start with the streets that it fronts. The street is by definition and necessity a place of public and commercial interchange, but modern architecture of the past 30 years has little by little eroded the street with open plazas and point block towers. While it was thought that the early buildings of the Modern Movement would, by virtue of these plazas, offer more light and air in the new 'hygienic city', the effect of such a strategy has been the erosion of the essence of urban definition. Its commercial and social life has been reduced and, in some cases, destroyed altogether.

Considering the openness of the sites surrounding the Humana building—the Belvedere and the river front, the plaza of the new Arts Center, and also the small 'park' behind the First National Tower—our site need not provide more of the same. On the contrary, we feel that our building should occupy the full site and re-establish the street edge, thereby restoring the sense of urban boundary as an important component of urban life. We have therefore brought the Humana building out to meet the sidewalk with an open shopping arcade along Fifth Street and a larger and more dominant public loggia on Main Street.

The main entrance to the building is through the public loggia along the sidewalk of Main Street. The colonnade holds the street edge with a rhythm and a scale that is sympathetic to the lower buildings adjoining it, while at the same time allowing free access to the loggia behind. This public entry space is dominated by a grand fountain where water cascades between the pilasters of a widely curving wall into a pool below. We felt that it was important that such a grand public gesture—an element of the building which was in a sense 'given back' to the city—should occur in a space which is open to the street and external to the semi-private realm of the inside lobby and office access. The sound of the fountain will make the large space inviting, while its embracing gesture to the Ohio River and the symbolic presence of the water itself will give thematic substance to this particular site. It is easy to imagine the people of the city occupying the concavity of the fountain place for a variety of activities, but especially using it for repose and contemplation during the day.

The covered commercial arcade, together with the public waterfall or fountain, attempts to engage the building with its urban site without any social or formal ambiguity. There have been numerous empty, open plazas and vacant interior atriums built in the recent past which have become a burden to cities, to building owners, and ultimately to the public at large. The rather crucial issues of private access and security may at times run counter to our interest in making public gestures in the interior of buildings. By excising the space beyond the street wall, by providing a curving, embracing formal gesture outside the building's interior, we feel that we have offset any ambiguity or misreading by the public and that the public will feel welcome by the fountain and the loggia and by the shopping arcade we have provided.

It was our aim that the Humana building should further contribute to its urban context by helping to mediate the disturbing disparity between the diminutive store fronts on Main Street and the enormity of the First National Tower. The stepback in the base floors, the scale of the colonnade of the loggia and the polychromy of its granite and Kasota stone facing relate to the existing storefronts, while the figural articulation of the crown on the top suggests a heightening of our building giving it

parity with the First National Tower. We felt that it was not necessary for our building to be literally as tall as the First National Tower in order to stand up to it. On the contrary, our contextual assimilation can be expected to give the Humana building a presence which its larger neighbour does not enjoy.

The Humana building itself is organised in three significant parts corresponding to the three distinct uses described by the programme. The specific requirements of the public and commercial spaces, of the offices, and of the Humana health club determined their location within the building, while the respective social and thematic character of the different activities informed their formal and figurative expression.

The base of the building contains the large public and commercial activities, as well as Humana's communal spaces such as the cafeteria which overlooks the Main Street loggia and the waterfall fountain. The portion of the building is represented externally by the colonnade which allows and expresses ready access from the street, while it maintains formal rapport with the adjacent store fronts on Main Street. The primary axis of the building moves through the centre of the fountain wall and into the building's lobby. The lobby's end wall will be elaborated by a mural or other art work whose theme relates to the Ohio River and Louisville. From this lobby, those entering the office building above will move from the central space to the side 'aisles', and finally to the high- and low-rise elevator banks located on the other side of the mural wall. The elevator lobby can also be reached through an entrance from Fifth Street.

The general office space is held within the body of the building above the 'base' floors and is expressed on the facades by separate windows which help relate the individual offices to the building mass. The four-and-a-half-foot-square windows are especially well scaled to the human body and are able to particularise the outside context as we stand at the aperture and look beyond its frame to the view. Openings of this size, which are more than adequate to light the interior, increase the energy efficiency of the building (as compared with 'window walls' for example), thereby saving operating costs.

The articulation of the centre of the Main Street facade expresses the vertical movement up through the building from the public spaces at the base, to the general offices, and eventually to the porch on the 24th floor. This porch, which bows out from the building in a gesture towards the river, affords space for a roof garden and a viewing terrace for the occupants of the building. The crown of our building is given over to the health and exercise club which is thought to be in part symbolic of the interest of Humana and therefore deserving of this special distinction. The various running and racquet activities held in the top of the building have access to the porch below which may also be used as an outdoor exercise area.

In its configuration, our Humana building is thought to have two fronts, one on Main Street, gesturing toward the river, and the other on the south side, looking back at downtown Louisville. On the south facade, sun rooms on each level of the building afford to the lobby areas light, orientation and views of the city.

In its contextual gesture, its visual stimulus and its urban amenities, the Humana building will contribute substantially to the revitalisation of the downtown riverfront sector of Louisville and act as a thematic catalyst for its redevelopment. Its aim is to restore to the area its former status as the vibrant business and commercial focus of the city, returning the city's human resources to the site of its historic beginnings.

Michael Graves

MICHAEL GRAVES
Sunar Furniture Showroom, Dallas, Texas, 1982

1 Entry loggia, or is it a piazza implied by the Egyptian piers?   2 Schinkelesque use of minimalist line; chairs uncanny, as Art Deco Biedermeier! (phs Charles McGrath)

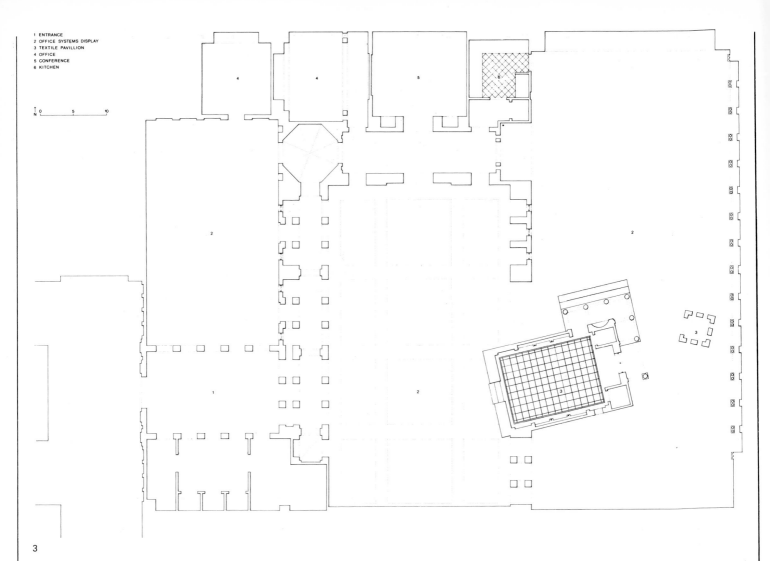

1 ENTRANCE
2 OFFICE SYSTEMS DISPLAY
3 TEXTILE PAVILLION
4 OFFICE
5 CONFERENCE
6 KITCHEN

3

3 Plan shows arcade used as semi-porous element.

4, 5 Lounge and side chair studies keep a Corbusian sculptural quality and combine it with Biedermeier detail.

6 Monumental table with pin-stripe look: almost a Neo-Classical formula. (ph Charles McGrath)

7, 8 Textile pavilions, open and closed, like Philip Johnson's adjacent Glass and Brick houses, but here treated as monumental abstraction. The 'Pompeian' columns are quite hallucinatory, as indeed are all the slightly veiled references. (phs Charles McGrath).

Volumetric Exaggeration

The Sunar showrooms that Graves has designed in several cities have given him an opportunity to develop an architectural language, just as stage-set design used to give to architects such as Inigo Jones. Most evident in Dallas is the development of the Hoffmann aesthetic—the linear, rectangular, atectonic frame punctuated by brass studs. A Graves table with fluted legs and upturned entablature, is very much in the Free Style Classical mode of Hoffmann c 1914. The thinness of line/heavy Egyptian pier is also a standard opposition. Indeed, one can find Egyptian qualities in the battered legs of the rather awkward Graves chair (reminiscent of those Wright designed for the Price Tower) and in the four-square piers—the hypostyle hall recurrent in many Sunar showrooms.

The highly figural abstraction, rather a contradiction in terms, is best seen in the loggia. Like Aldo Rossi's Modena cemetery, this is a hieratic and still space, but drenched from above with a white light. The textile pavilions—set pieces collaged in an open plan—are even more figural: a closed aedicule and open colonnade. Some may feel the piers have become so gargantuan they are now really walls that shrink the pyramidal roof in size. Indeed, coupled with the ultra-thin colonettes, they are, no doubt, Mannerist distortions of a classical convention. But as with all such distortions, they recall memories without specifying them; in this suggestion lies their hallucinatory power.

Pompeii, for instance, is recalled by the dark colouring and twinned colonettes—surmounted, however, by a capital of a golden light bulb! Finally, the boudoir may be an appropriate image for Sunar, especially as it has improved sales in the past; here one feels it needs some contrast and tension to heighten its softness. CJ

The Dallas showroom is organised to allow the visitor to view the furniture groups and systems while maintaining a sense of orientation and place. Architectural or perceptual devices are used to assist movement through the showroom by making linear linkages connecting the various furniture groupings. The middle display area is established as the central compositional figure by virtue of its location within the plan and the articulation of its enclosing surfaces. The strength of this room allows for the idiosyncracies of its perimeter which in turn intensify its reading as a central figure. The primary axis of this display area is terminated by a wall mural within the conference room which attempts to recapture significant elements of the themes used within the architectural composition itself. The showroom includes two separate pavilions within the larger enclosure that contain the textile collection. These pavilions are placed in such a way as to distinguish them as more romantic or picturesque elements within a larger landscape.

Michael Graves

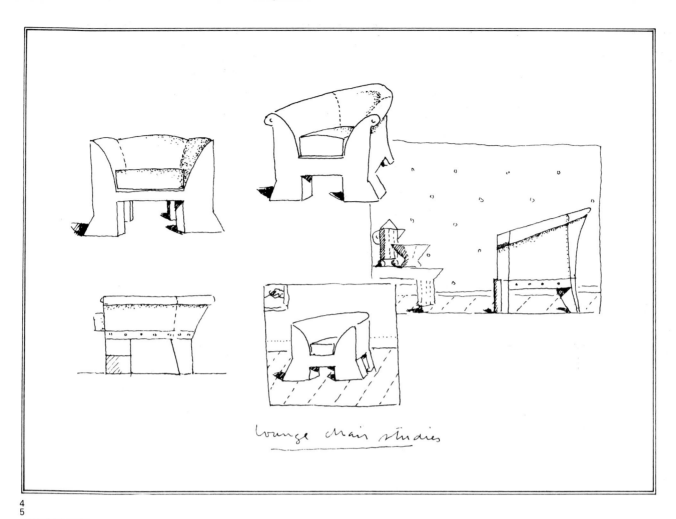

lounge chair studies

4
5

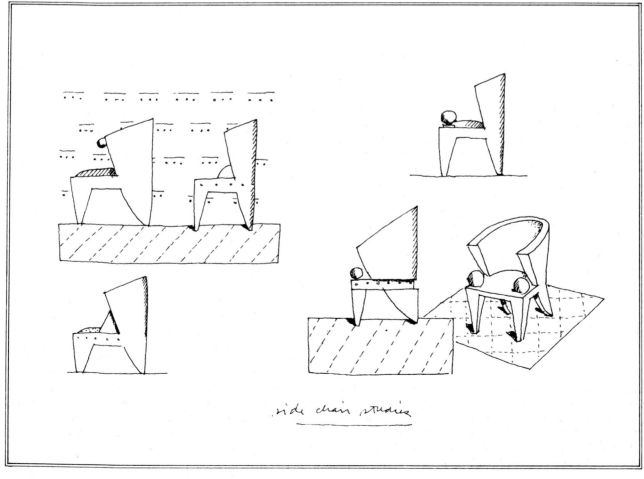

side chair studies

7
8

HANS HOLLEIN

Städtiches Museum Abteiberg, Mönchengladbach, 1976–82

The Museum as Acropolis

The museum has now emerged as the pre-eminent building type of this century. Temple, church, town hall, skyscraper, new university—these have previously been the protagonists of architecture, holding the institutions which have sanctioned architecture as an art. But their power has dwindled with their declining credibility. Few citizens celebrate politics in the age of television candidates; few faithful have survived the commercialisation of religion. A chronic recession has dampened socialist, as much as capitalist, ardour and it is said that New Yorkers are no longer interested in sex. Even worse, they're bored by gossip.

What survives this near-total agnosticism? A belief, however hesitant, in the role of the artist, in the unfolding of present-day culture, in the immanent expression of the soulless spirit, the wanderings of the unrestrained intellect and imagination, the vagaries of the Modern Zeitgeist. Collections of Modern art are still built up with a consuming personal faith; or at least a belief in the exchange value of art. The Modern artist such as Joseph Beuys is still regarded with the kind of awe primitive societies reserve for the shaman. If he doesn't provide an incomprehensible epigram (or a three-hour performance) on the state of Modern society, Reaganomics and brotherhood, we feel cheated. As Matthew Arnold observed long ago, art is becoming the new religion, and this means, for architects, that the new museum is its cathedral.

The first museum buildings (as opposed to single galleries) did not resemble cathedrals, or even churches, but were rather a cross between temple and palazzo. Soane's Dulwich (1811),

Von Klenze's Glyptothek (1815), Schinkel's Altes Museum (1823), and Smirke's British Museum (1823), all had that peculiar Neo-Classical mixture. It might be a temple front plus long gallery wall, as in the Glyptothek, or the implication of a temple order tied to an arcade, as in the case of Dulwich, but most of the early museums had a hierarchical set of rectangular rooms—the temple cella—pivoting around a central arrival point—the grand salon of the palace. The reasons were various. First, Durand had fixed the type in a functional way as the addition of measured, top-lit units, organised on axes around a central rotunda (Précis, 1802–09). Secondly, the palace and temple had a specific architectural solemnity befitting to a public collection. Lastly, the associations were correct: what was right to house the Athenian treasures was right to house the Elgin Marbles, what was suitable for the Medici collections was proper for the national patrons, whether Ludwig I or, later, Queen Victoria.

This 'temple palace' type dominated well into the twentieth century until Frank Lloyd Wright challenged it with his enigmatic sculptural whirlpool, the Guggenheim Museum (1959)—almost the first of many mysterious objects which, windowless, relate

1 The Acropolis, Athens. The volumes shift in importance as one ascends the zig-zag path; the Parthenon, dramatic culmination, goes in and out of view. (ph Jencks)
2 Hans Hollein, Israel Verkehrsbüro, Vienna, 1979–80. Palm trees on a grid of sand surround an oasis of water. Eroded nature set against right-angled culture is an old convention which Hollein has made particularly his own.
3 Hans Hollein, Perchtoldsdorf Town Hall, Austria, 1975–76. Chrome seats and grid are set against marble grid and stylised grapes and vine—all put together with a craftsmanlike precision. (ph Jerzy Surwillo)

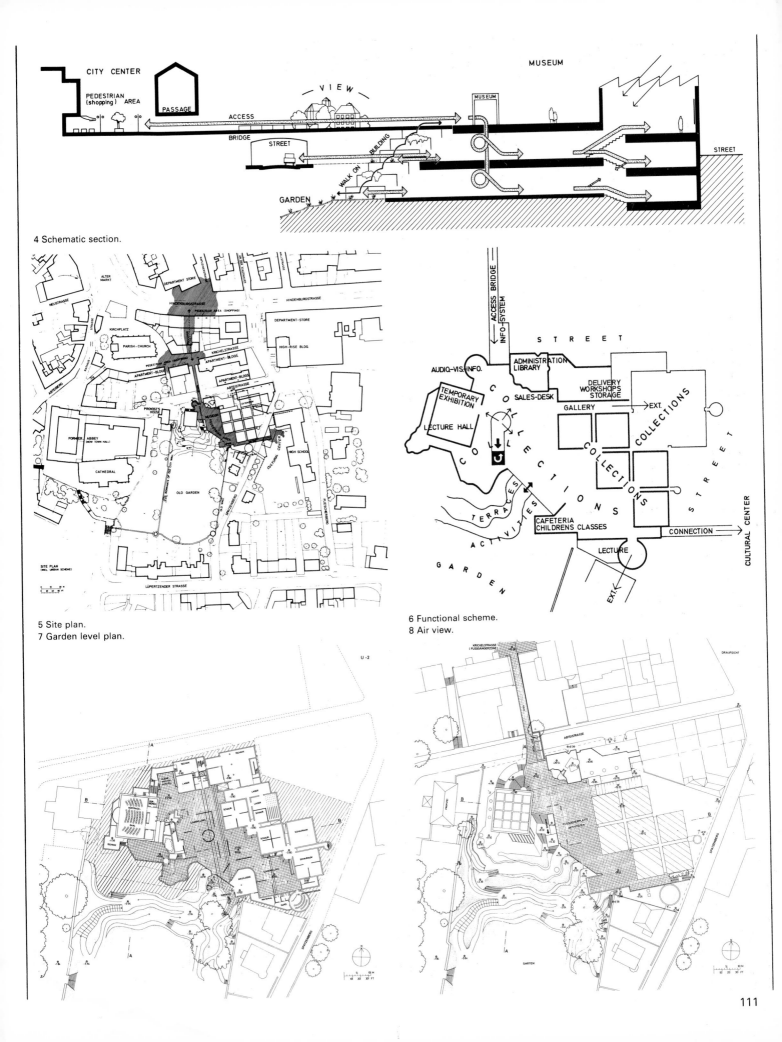

CITY CENTER

PEDESTRIAN (shopping) AREA

PASSAGE

VIEW

MUSEUM

MUSEUM

ACCESS

BRIDGE

STREET

STREET

BUILDING

WALK ON

GARDEN

4 Schematic section.

5 Site plan.
7 Garden level plan.

6 Functional scheme.
8 Air view.

ACCESS BRIDGE
INFO-SYSTEM

STREET

AUDIO-VIS-INFO.

ADMINISTRATION
LIBRARY

DELIVERY
WORKSHOPS
STORAGE

TEMPORARY
EXHIBITION

SALES-DESK

GALLERY

EXT.

COLLECTIONS

LECTURE HALL

COLLECTIONS

COLLECTIONS

COLLECTIONS

STREET

TERRACES

ACTIVITIES

CAFETERIA
CHILDRENS CLASSES

CONNECTION

CULTURAL CENTER

LECTURE

GARDEN

EXT.

111

9 The 'Propylaeum' dominates the top piazza which is almost itself a temenos, or sacred enclosure, bounded by a wall. The Propylaea on the Acropolis actually had a painting gallery. (ph Jencks)

10 The 'Propyleum' or main gate at night with the theatre in the background and the galeries below right. (ph Hollein)

11 The 'square painting' of the cathedral is framed in aluminium squares—a witty transformation of the environment into an art object. (ph Jencks)

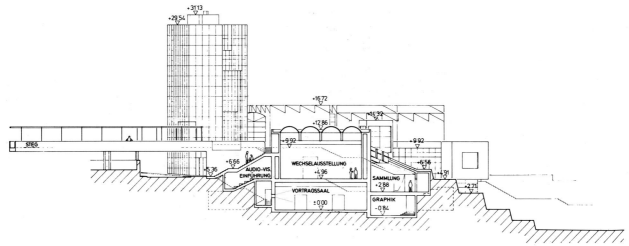

12-14 Sections

not at all to the urban context. The point of the Late-Modern Museum, as Breuer knew well, is to be a startling contrast, a magnificent non sequitur *like a John Cage silence, the Cattle-Prod, as well as Shock of the New.* I M Pei's monumental East Wing of Washington's National Gallery (1978) induces the kind of insensate euphoria Freud once described as the Great Oceanic Feeling. The disjunctive epiphany, in cultural terms a church of miracles, remains one model for the museum, which we often see realised as the sculptural monument. The other is exemplified in the Pompidou Centre with its isotropic loft space, conceptually a warehouse and superior supermarket. Thus two basic functional and two associational types remain as an uneasy amalgam for today's museum: the monument/warehouse and the temple/cathedral. It is Hollein's virtue that he has seen through these implicit codes and combined all four in his acropolis.

Fragmentation of Types

The entrance to the Museum, supposing you approach it from the city of Mönchengladbach, is understated to the point of obscurity: my taxi driver missed it despite a very explicit map. At the moment, it consists of an almost unmarked pedestrian bridge leading to the 'piazza' or 'rooftop', which in turn leads to the 'Propylaeum', which is indeed the unmistakable gateway. This does not have a classical pediment, but like Le Corbusier's similar pavilion-entrance to the Salvation Army, there are no doubts about its function. Stainless-steel column, white marble, geometry, placement—all announce as strongly as a triumphal arch the beginning. In this space, both 'Propylaeum' and 'Temple of Nike', a lighting fixture is carved like the Victory of Samothrace to underline the associations with the Acropolis, but

as is the case with all my terms in inverted commas, so far and to follow, the associations are indirect and fragmented. In fact the building, designed in 1972 and finished ten years later, is a labyrinth of veiled associations, and fragmented types. If the references appear more than usually hidden, it is a consequence of this time lag. They are, however, nonetheless present.

Crowning the scheme is an eroded tower, the administrative head which wags the sprawling body and tail. It's a four-square, rectangular block with sandstone stereometry and then two ripples of glass—one which falls out to the north, the other which breaks back to the south, the garden and view. Conceptually, this embodies the fundamental opposition between nature (curved and eroded) and culture (right-angled and complete) that will be taken up elsewhere—primarily in the 'vineyards' terraced down the hill, versus the square galleries. We recognise this tower: a flat-top office, a glass, steel and masonry business centre. The type may be fragmented, but it is no less identifiable for that.

The same is true of the saw-toothed galleries towards which we first descend under the 'Propylaeum'. These are top-lit rooms, familiar since Soane's Dulwich Picture Gallery, but made slightly odd by combination with the north-facing zig-zag lighting of a factory. Saw-toothed boxes, modified perhaps from Stirling and Gowan's Leicester University Engineering Building, were later strung out by Stirling in a classical U-shape around his Stuttgart Museum. Both Stirling and Hollein promote the regeneration of classical culture by its combination with industrial realism. If we expect seven galleries under the seven boxes we are partly surprised, for what happens is a rather complex set of combined types resulting in further fragmentation.

Only five of the boxes shelter defined squares, and these are

13

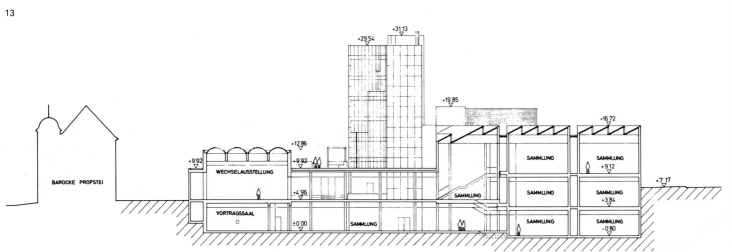

114

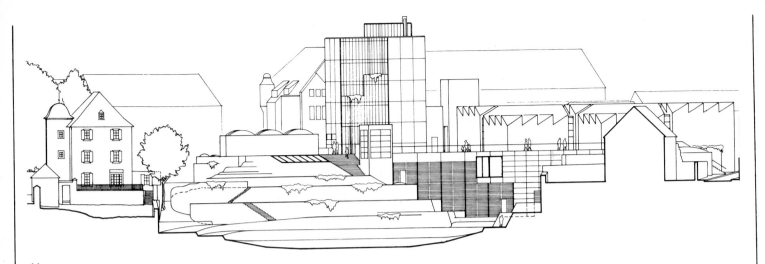

14

traversed, against all expectations on the diagonal. The remaining two are placed above free-flowing, double-height open space. This provides a combination of warehouse/temple which is encountered after the descent from the entrance. It is momentarily confusing; indeed, one might think, surveying the ambiguous white space unfolding in all directions, that it is as formless as the history of Modern Art: no beginning, middle or end, all a wandering search dependent on sensation and the imminent development of an idea. The fact that a few inscrutable Beuys and further abstractions of André, Judd and Serra fan out in all directions only confirms the suspicion. This, the European MOMA, appears at first like an endless rambling narrative. Happily, however, it's a 'second-glance' architecture which is always disconfirming, or modifying, an initial hypothesis.

On the top floor is a relatively traditional set of rooms which allow large canvases and sculpture to be seen in a stable atmosphere. The view across diagonals, an idea which relates this to Dutch Structuralist works of the 1960s, focuses on sculpture placed centrally in the square. At the same time one can focus obliquely on the huge paintings of, for instance, Frank Stella. Thus a double order is immediately apparent—two grids shifted at 45°—which gives a new life to the basically classical room.

Modern artists generally want the mixture of spatial types Hollein has provided: large and small, formal and informal, flexible and permanent, foreground and background. Indeed, the dialectic between these fragmented types is the obvious answer to the varied requirements of Modern Art—so obvious that one wonders why recent museums have not institutionalised it already, or conversely why they have remained immured in a monosemantic type.

15 South elevation

Generally speaking, the Mönchengladbach Museum develops a typically Post-Modern space with its varied set of cues: indistinct boundaries, skews and diagonals, ambiguous or overlapping orders, layering, surprise, contrast and dramatic movement—almost every spatial convention of Post-Modernism is here. The Modern free plan, where it does exist, is actually incorporated within a set of other orders—circular stair platforms and column and wall grids. Where rotated grids don't mesh, or where superincumbent stairs are rotated away from each other, there is a left-over poché space. One of these 'Expressionist' spaces was originally intended to show painters from that school. Unfortunately, however, this initial semantic matching of space to art was not followed through, and we do not quite have the nineteenth-century personalised museum with the rooms tailor-made for the objects. Rather, there is a rich system of differences within a white aesthetic.

As one explores further and further into the building, finally reaching under the undulating 'vineyards' on one side, or theatre and enclosed squares on the other, a growing impression is confirmed. The building has, if not one ending, then several culminations; if not one ordered sequence, then three or four distinct routes. This overlapping of separate orders is particularly appropriate to Modern Art, which often consists in the transformation of singular traditions or separate concepts: De Stijl into Geometric and Hard Edge Abstraction, Suprematism into Minimalism and Concepual Art, and so forth. There is no single plot to Modern Art, just as there is no guiding patronage, or iconographic programme. It is all imminent development—follow the inherent visual or conceptual idea—without necessarily a beginning or termination, without hierarchy or (much) value judgement. The 'sieve' space of Hollein, the mul-

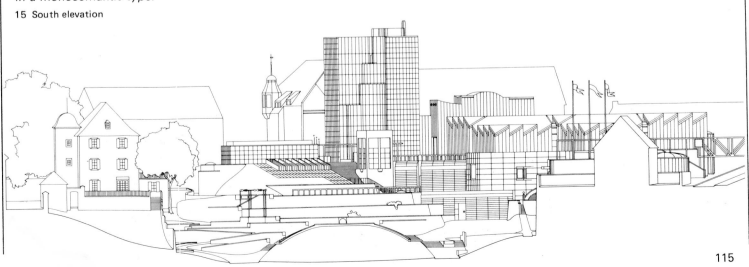

17 Gridded sections of lights and structure appropriate to minimalist Late-Modern painting and sculpture within. Hollein's eclecticism articulates different epochs and styles of Modernism. (ph Jencks)

◀ 16 The 'column/wall' pair provides a psychological stability and backdrop, but some of them can also be moved—hence a certain flexibility. The artists and director find this dialectic appealing. (ph Jencks)

18 Steps down from the entrance to a platform-'stylobate'. (ph Jencks)

19   20

tidirectional routes, allows these coherent avenues to be followed in their meandering criss-cross, and yet at the same time
and quite surprisingly it also manages to achieve beginnings,
middles and several ends.

It isn't until we have traversed the site to the bottom garden
and then retraced our steps up the zig-zag path, catching reflections of fragments in mirrorplate, that the overall conception
becomes entirely clear. For now the Acropolis image is compelling. The cafeteria, a pristine rectangle of polished aluminium, juts out aggressively, a temple set at right angles to
the 'Propylaeum'. As we climb this acropolis, four main rectangles alternate in counterpoint, set off as they are against each
other. Some are obliquely placed—an Erectheum against the
Parthenon—to compress space, but all these flat-topped forms
are fragments of whole figures, not totally free-standing monuments. However, like the temple on the Acropolis they come
into view and disappear, dramatically, as one climbs the hill. If
there is no single Parthenon to cap this architectural promenade
then that, once again, merely underscores the pluralism of an
art form where no single orthodoxy rules or dominates.

Influence and Abstraction
This, Hollein's first building of any size and civic importance,
has been a long time in the making. Economic uncertainties
have held it up, but throughout this long period its director,
Johannes Cladders, in a sense the real patron of the building,
has played a significant role. Without his continued support,
and detailed advice, the museum would not be the finely tuned
instrument that it is. The organisation of the collection and
rooms, the variety of lighting systems, the 'syntax of options',
were all worked out and discussed with him. If his influence
can be felt, so can that of a host of architects. The difficulty of
determining this influence is caused by the protracted period of

19 The *Victory of Samothrace* is implicitly recalled by adopting her curves and
wings into the curve of the lighting fixture; here Hollein allows himself one
ornament that refers to the Athenian prototype. (ph Jencks)

design, which resulted in mutual borrowings back and forth.
But no doubt the strength of the museum results from the
richness of architectural ideas. And these have a necessary
history. Aside from the building types already mentioned, we
find the sources predominantly Modernist.

The tower, for instance, has an eroded cut reminiscent of
Aalto's gentle undulations, Stirling's cascade of glass at Leicester and Hollein's own previous erosions. The violent opposition
between stereometric sandstone and mirrorplate, between
honey-coloured masonry and glass and steel, is reminiscent of
Le Corbusier's strong juxtapositions. Violent contrasts, concor-
dia violentes, heighten the presence of each part, a rhetoric of
opposites developed equally by Charles Moore and his theory
of the architectural geode (hard and tough outside, soft and
sparkling inside). No doubt the tower is a geode too, but the
crystalline insides which are broken apart also spill over the top
of the building to the other side.

These contrast with what is, effectively, another current
preoccupation—the abstract gridded wall, either in sandstone
or polished aluminium. The former is reminiscent of Le Corbusier's stereometric schemes of the 1930s as well as of much
Schinkelesque work today, while the latter relates to Richard
Meier's and Arata Isozaki's grey gridded buildings. To trace an
influence on Stirling's Stuttgart Museum, or Isozaki's Kitakyu-
shu Museum (which has similar square jutting windows held
inside grids) is perhaps to miss the point since the scheme was
developed over the many years this solution-type was in the
air. It does mean, however, that today it seems a little less fresh
than it would have been six years ago, when such forms were
first built. Time has slightly blunted the cutting edge that these

21

20 Galleries are top-lit by factory lighting, and covered with a zinc which will take on a darker tone with time. (ph Jencks)
21 Aerial view (photomontage).

shapes originally had.

The same is also true of the diagonal, Structuralist organisation worked out by Louis Kahn and certain Dutch architects in the mid-1960s, when the motif was an exciting violation of the corner, and a practical principle of in-between space. Today at Mönchengladbach it is a more proven formula. What is lost in freshness is, however, regained in maturity. The diagonal grid of the top floors, for instance, is made more emphatic by the diagonal factory lighting which sets up clear binary oppositions between each grid.

Whether Stirling's Stuttgart Museum owes its skylights and pedestrian way to this building, or whether Hollein owes his experiments in light and space to Louis Kahn's Fort Worth, is a speculation of small importance compared to the central question: does the architect transform his sources and prove them in the present context? Certainly here there is no diminution of expressive strength, and the consummate Hollein detailing is up to Stirling's and Kahn's. In the handling of marble, slick-tech and lighting equipment, it is even superior to its progenitors, perhaps due to Hollein's long experience with interior design at a small scale. Most of his previous work, since his early Retti Candle Shop of 1965, has been precious interior detailing.

The question of transforming sources is best considered as a consequence of abstraction. Square, rectangle, saw-tooth ridge, flat roof, undecorated steel column—all the elements have been used in an archetypal way so that they recall not so much any particular building, but a general type. Memory of previous architecture is no doubt involved in the conception and perception, but it is always kept at the most fundamental level. Personally, I would have preferred one or two explicit

signs to heighten this implicit symbolism—perhaps some specific icon on the tower top (as an Art Nouveau architect such as Olbrich might have attempted). After all this is as powerful a building type as the cathedral next door with its spires, and it seems wrong that the twentieth century can't declare the faith in art which it so much betrays. But perhaps this muteness is caused by the social uncertainty of art as religion, and also by the fact that the building was designed before Post-Modernism became self-confident with iconic gestures.

Even without explicit signs and ornament, it will probably become recognised as the significant breakthrough it is: one of the first new museums to encompass a variety of spaces, lighting conditions and exhibition attitudes into a dialectic. Variety, flexibility, pluralism—the clichés of the 1960s—have not recently produced great museums because the architect has become too enthralled by a formal or repetitive solution to these very legitimate demands. They have produced monuments, or loft spaces, or essentially monosemantic designs. Instead, here at Mönchengladbach, they receive an abstract, eclectic solution, one that relies on opposition as a method, and one which is particularly detailed, carried through by someone who clearly loves built architecture. The Acropolis with its sacred enclosure, its votive columns, statues, stoas, and treasuries, was also a place where art was worshipped. The Propylaea had the Pinacotheca, the Parthenon its statue by Phidias; the whole, ancient stronghold hovered on its rugged hill as a Doric 'sign of reason'. Hollein's subdued classicism also contrasts its quiet dignity with a moving landscape; perhaps after all this acropolis of art is a rather inevitable culmination of an agnostic age.

CJ